THERE'S NO STANDING STILL

How to Grow a Profitable Dental Practice Focusing on You, Your People and Your Patients

DR. SEAN MOHTASHAMI

There's No Standing Still – How to Grow a Profitable Dental Practice Focusing on You, Your People, and Your Patients.

eBook ISBN: 978-1-958405-96-3
Paperback ISBN: 978-1-958405-94-9
Hardcover ISBN: 978-1-958405-95-6
Ingram Spark ISBN: 978-1-962570-03-9
Library of Congress Control Number: 2023915873
Printed in the United States of America

Interior Design: Marigold2k
Contributing Authors: Julieanne O'Connor, Steve Sperry, Steven Rowell
Published By: Spotlight Publishing House
https://spotlightpublishinghouse.com

www.4MDentalimplants.com
https://4Minstitute.com

Disclaimer

We are not affiliated, associated, authorized, endorsed by, or in any way officially connected with The Walt Disney Company, Disney Enterprises, Inc., or any of its subsidiaries or its affiliates. The official Disney web site is available at www.disney.com. All Disney parks, attractions, lands, shows, event names, etc. are registered trademarks of The Walt Disney Company.

Walt Disney World® is a registered trademark of The Walt Disney Company. This website, TheresNoStandingStill.com, and the book *There's No Standing Still: How to Grow a Profitable Dental Practice Focusing on You, Your Patients, and Your Practice,* refers to various Disney copyrighted trademarks, characters, marks and registered marks owned by the Walt Disney Company, Disney Enterprises, Inc., and other trademark owners. The use in this website and/or in the book of trademarked names and images is strictly for editorial purposes, and no commercial claim to their use, or suggestion of sponsorship or endorsement, is made by the authors or publisher. Those words or terms that the authors and publisher have reason to believe are trademarks are designated as such by the use of initial capitalization, where appropriate. However, no attempt has been made to identify or designate all words or terms to which trademark or other proprietary rights may exist. Nothing contained herein is intended to express a judgment on, or affect the validity of legal status of, any word or term as a trademark, service mark, or other proprietary mark.

Endorsements

As someone who has had the privilege of being mentored by Dr. Sean for the past three years, I can confidently say that his book is a game-changer for dental professionals. Dr. Sean's guidance and expertise have transformed not only my own practice but also the way I approach patient care and leadership in dentistry. This book is a true reflection of his wisdom, passion, and dedication to helping others succeed, and I am grateful for the insights and strategies it offers. If you are looking for a mentor in the dental profession, I wholeheartedly recommend Dr. Sean's book as a roadmap to achieving personal and professional growth as you envision it!

Alex D. Lopez, DDS Periodontist

As a dentist and a dedicated professional committed to supporting fellow dental practitioners, this book serves as compelling evidence that the realm of practice ownership encompasses far more than the teachings of dental school. It's a valuable resource for anyone in the field.

—**Dr. Len Tau**, Founder, Tau Dental Consulting, Host of *The Raving Patients Podcast*

This indispensable book is an essential companion for dentists aiming to elevate their influence and grow their practice. As a multi-practice owner now, I wish I had had a book like this when starting out in my career.

—**Jedediah V. Huss** DDS, DICOI, Owner/Founder/Clinical Director of Restored Smiles, LLC

As an oral surgeon and practice owner, I understand the allure of growth, while also recognizing the necessity of establishing systems and honing soft skills to translate that ambition into reality. Dr. Sean's book is essential reading for those seeking expansion while preserving their quality of life.

—**Daniel Yang** DDS, MD

There's No Standing Still is packed with invaluable insights on establishing and managing a successful dental practice or group of practices. It is humanized with introspection and emphasizes patient satisfaction, team synergy, and operational excellence.

—**Aurelio Sahagun**, Executive Vice President – Head of North America – Straumann Group

You get the sense starting from Chapter 1 that Dr. Sean's wisdom is from his own personal experience with challenges through trial and error. This book can serve as a leisurely read as a biography, an inspirational bible, or a reference guide for your career. An all-around book. Just like Dr. Sean. The all-around author, clinician, father, and businessman.

—**Marcus Ji Hoon Hwang**, DDS, MD, Oral &
Maxillofacial Surgeon

Dr. Sean Mohtashami's book, *"There's No Standing Still,"* is a valuable resource for dentists seeking to improve their professional journey. Chapters 5 and 6, authored by respected coach and lecturer Julieanne O'Connor, delve into achieving success while maintaining a quality life and the power of influence, emphasizing trust and credibility. This book provides essential insights for dentists aiming to excel in their practice and personal development.

—**Michael Keeter**, Director of Business Development, Avadent, 16+ Years in Dentistry, Connection Strategist

After spending my entire professional career in various sectors of dentistry, which is 28 years in the making, I can with great confidence share that this book explicitly captures the tools for success for any DSO leader or dental practice owner. One thing I learned many years ago is that there is no need to reinvent the wheel when recreating success, rather, there is a real opportunity to learn from the valuable experiences gained from the trials and turbulations of those "who have been there". In the book, There's No Standing Still, the author shares his real-life stories with authenticity and provides gentle guidance, so we don't have to learn the same lessons the hard way. Not only does the author address all the fundamentals of practice ownership but they also provide key guidance with actionable steps on how to address the root issues that lead to provider burnout, staff turnover and patient experience.

—**Ellie Naderi**, CEO, Oral Health United

Dr. Sean's book, *There's No Standing Still* is full of insights and expertly presented information. It's a must-read for anyone passionate about dentistry." Gustavo Campos, American Denta Institute.

—**Dr. Gustavo Campos**, American Dental Institute

For every dental practice owner, this invaluable book offers a wealth of smart strategies with takeaways an owner can put into practice right away.

—**Sean Ebrahimian** DDS, FICOI

This book offers immense value to clinicians, both seasoned professionals and those in the early stages of their careers, in numerous aspects. Dr. Sean adeptly presents an unparalleled and all-encompassing methodology for establishing and expanding your desired practice and team. The personal touch he brings to this book introduces a level of value that surpasses any prior experience.

—**Athena Goodarzi**, DDS, Lead Educator 4M Institute

It's been close to 30 years since I met Dr Sean for the first time! Yikes we're getting old! We were sitting across from one another in dental school for the first couple years. You get to know someone pretty well during those very harsh, formative years. We hit it off pretty much right from the start and I have considered him a class act ever since.

He was always a multi-tasker from those early days. Even with a crazy schedule of back-to-back classes and labs, he always managed to squeeze in a workout, or just take some time to recharge by the pool. We always used to say he looks like he just got back from vacation due to his year-round suntan glow!

After graduating, Sean did the unthinkable by taking and actually passing the crazy-impossible Nevada dental boards. After dominating Nevada for a few years, he did what would be considered crazy, and came back to his roots in the very saturated Los Angeles dental market. Amazingly, he just continued to grow and grow as a person, as well as a successful dentist. I credit his meteoric rise all these years to several things.

I think first and foremost, he is genuinely a nice guy. He doesn't have ulterior motives, and when you talk to him, as a person, or as your dentist, there's a trusting quality under the cool, confident personality. I am always impressed seeing how he is so loved by his ever-expanding team of doctors and dental team all the way down to the vendors and labs he works with.

Second, Dr Sean has energy up the wazoo! This guy is on the move from the moment he wakes up for an early workout, all the way to making it to all his daughters' dance recitals, birthday parties, and endless school functions. In the middle of all this, he still manages to have a life of his own. He manages to do and be all of this, while still remaining unbelievably humble, approachable, and willing to learn. It's very easy for one to lose touch with reality once you have reached a certain level of success. It's Dr Sean's ability to continue to strive for the next level without ever becoming too complacent that makes him a true standout. He is a true asset to the field of dentistry, as well as a true gentleman and a dear friend to me! I feel I want to be better when I am around such a person.

—**Ramin Moradi**, D.D.S

THERE'S NO STANDING STILL

How to Grow a Profitable Dental Practice Focusing on You, Your People and Your Patients

DR. SEAN MOHTASHAMI

SPOTLIGHT
PUBLISHING HOUSE
Goodyear, Arizona

Contents

Introduction

I wrote this book to save you ten years of strife, struggle, stress, overwhelm, burnout, and *trial by fire.* I am forever grateful for what I learned in dental school, the mentors who shaped my thinking and guided me along the way, and the clinical skills I gained. However, there is so much more to the reality of what it takes to succeed as a dentist, an entrepreneur, and a good human being.

Throughout this book, you have learned what works well for successful dental practices and precisely what you can do to achieve excellence and build the life you want and deserve while transforming lives daily. However, this book wouldn't be complete if I didn't share insights from my years of building multiple profitable practices. Profit is not the only purpose for what we do day-in and day-out. Profit is an engine that fuels our continued success. Profit reflects our ability to provide exceptional value and quality outcomes at a fair price while also managing our business and leading our people in ways that enable us to build a company that matters. A company that exists as much for the family of team members within it as it does for the patients it serves.

Whether you want to keep your solo-practice healthy and growing or you want to build your own large DSO, having a compelling purpose beyond *making money* is what will help you weather the storms of tough times and find meaning in what you are doing for yourself, your people, and your patients.

Leading and managing profitable dental practices has given me a family of more than 100 team members and nine practices by the end of this year. Starting with Las Vegas, we have added Anaheim Hills, Long Beach, Newport Beach, Murrieta, Valencia, Palm Desert, Riverside, and San Diego. We now perform several thousand All-on-4 procedures and hundreds of restorative and cosmetic procedures yearly.

Most important to me are the 100+ team members because we have no patients without them. I consider these great people my extended family. I am so proud and grateful to hear when one of my team members can buy their first car, or their first home, can get a much-needed surgery or treatment, finish their degree, start college, go on vacation for the first time in years, or support their parents in transition. Over the years, it has been a thrill to see team members start in entry-level positions who are now in critical roles at levels of our organization.

My hope for you is that you will find meaning and purpose in building a company and a team that transforms the lives of your patients. I hope you now see the potential in yourself, your people, your patients, and your practice! And most of all, always remember...

There's no standing still!

You

CHAPTER 1

Building Blocks for Personal Success

"Every day, I want to become a better 'me' in some way."
—Dr. Sean Mohtashami

Walking to my gate in the Las Vegas airport…

"Let me get your shoes shined. They're going to look great!"

I hear it again.

"Sir, let me get your shoes shined. They're going to look great!"

I pause and turn to see a gentleman looking up at me, with wrinkles from a well-lived life and hands worn from years of doing what he loves. His hands clenched tightly to each end of a soft, clean cloth. He's buffing a man's shoes, like a man on a mission. Yet not too busy to give me a reassuring smile and a nod that said, "Take a seat and rest your feet."

His energy and laugh were infectious, as if he didn't have a care in the world. His eyes were sharply attuned to the meticulous duty at hand, buffing the other man's shoes to a perfect shine.

"Wow, this guy is really good," I thought. "He loves what he's doing, and he loves how he does it even more."

As he begins to shine my shoes, he's working so hard; his sweaty bald head shines, and his smile fills the terminal. He finishes my shoes and looks at them like a proud papa seeing his first baby boy.

It's $14. I tell him to keep the change. And he runs through the crowd of passengers, with my $20 bill stuck to his sweaty forehead. He joyfully yells, "Another successful customer!" The crowd erupts in cheers and clapping.

This shoe shiner man is successful… extremely successful! He takes pride in what he does and how he does it. He delights his customers. And his passion spreads joy to the people all around him.

It's not about the money for him. It's about how he can make a difference in people's lives, and shining shoes is just a bonus.

It's not what you do that determines your success. It's how you do it.

I've been inspired by so many people from all walks of life. I've learned so much from others throughout my life. We all have our own life story to tell. When we share our stories with one another, we begin to understand and see one another. Later in this book, you will see how this has changed my own life and the lives of our patients. Perhaps sharing some of my stories will help you understand my journey and why I've written this book for you.

My Own Journey

Growing up in Tehran, Iran, with three older brothers, I witnessed my father work tirelessly in his print shop and eventually develop an import-export business. His incredible work ethic was unparalleled. He always managed to stay motivated, despite the struggles he faced. Today, at 87, he still works every day.

My father's inspiring story began at the age of 12 when he left his hometown of Kashan, Iran. He rented a room from his oldest sister and worked in a print shop, making only a penny a day. Through sheer determination, he eventually bought his own printer and opened his own little shop, which grew into a successful professional print shop. When I was 9, I would go to work with my dad. He instilled in me the importance of managing money and working hard.

Growing up in Iran during the revolution, my family experienced the harsh realities of war and government unrest. One day, during the Iranian Revolution, my father held my hand as we walked down the sidewalk, and suddenly gunshots rang out all around us. People started running and shouting. My dad said, "Let's go!" He picked me up as we ran, and we heard more gunfire. Then I saw a man get shot right in front of me. We didn't stop. We had to keep running. In that sudden moment, I was shown how precious life truly is.

My family's stories are influenced dramatically by the reality of war. Two of my three brothers were unable to leave the country due to their military service, and I witnessed firsthand the brutal impact of wartime injuries on my cousin. My oldest brother had already been in the US for a few years. He came to America for treatment of a heart condition. My parents had a different life plan in mind for me.

Getting to America

In March 1985, my father presented me with my passport and told me he was taking me to Istanbul, Turkey, on our way to America. Despite my eagerness to leave, I was full of apprehension when the time came to depart. Upon arriving in America, my father stayed with me for two months and then returned to Iran. At age 15, I stayed with an American family as an exchange student to experience the culture and learn English quickly.

My father insisted that I skip two grades of high school, which made me the smallest kid in my class, unable to communicate in English, and left me feeling lonely and disconnected from my 17-year-old classmates. But I persevered, driven by the memory of the sacrifices my family made to get me to America. I didn't want to disappoint them. This is the biggest reason I was able to navigate the hard times of high school and not let it break me.

I learned quickly...

"

If I want to make it,
be successful,
and make a big difference
in the world,
there is no standing still.

"

Importance of Humility

My home was always filled with warmth and the aromas of my mother's delicious Persian cooking. As a house mom, my mother dedicated her days to caring for our family of four boys, and she did it all with genuine humility and deep religious faith. From her, I learned valuable lessons in humility, commitment, and generosity.

Alongside my family, Shotokan Karate played a significant role in shaping who I am today. Under the guidance of my Shotokan master instructor, Sensei Greg, martial arts taught me to control my emotions and reactions and to remain humble in my never-ending pursuit of excellence. As I progressed through the martial arts ranks, earning new colored belts, I remained grounded in the knowledge that there is always more to be learned and ways to improve. I am forever grateful for my brother Hamid and his insistence and inspiration to practice martial arts.

Thanks to the influence of my mother's unwavering faith and my pursuit of excellence through martial arts, I have learned to appreciate the human side of things, remain humble, be self-reliant, and strive to be a good person.

LESSONS LEARNED

These lessons have stayed with me all these years. In fact, as a business owner and leader, I found sharing my beliefs and guiding principles with my teams goes a long way in building trust and understanding between us. Here are several principles for success and simply being a good human:

No Standing Still

My parents taught me to always keep moving forward, no matter my situation. Hard work and hustle are in my DNA. It is the way I see the world.

I often ask my team members, students, and mentees, "If you are going to spend eight hours working each workday, and you want to learn and grow, then why not work hard and hustle?" Yet "never standing still" is also about "never settling," not succumbing to the cancer of complacency.

I believe one of the secrets to our success is the work culture we have fostered in our collective and individual pursuits of excellence. Today, our team members inspire, encourage, and support one another to work hard and hustle for our patients, our people, and our practice. Throughout this book, you will discover several ways this was achieved and how we keep our culture from waning.

Generous Giving Without Expectations

It has been my experience that there are three types of people... Givers, Takers, and Exchangers. I truly believe in my own life, and in observing other successful people over the years, most successful people are Givers—without expectations. Takers often sadly struggle. Exchangers give, yet with expectations of fair trade, quid pro quo.

Giving must be done with no expectations for reciprocation from others. This is easier said than done. My daily goal is to seek ways to be generous and kind without expectations of anything in return. My three daughters have inspired me greatly along the way by giving me love, loving life, and enjoying every bit of what they have without wanting more. They are grateful for every little thing I have given them.

No Ego

Learning humility came from seeing my parents' consistent actions over many years, not by words alone. When I see a piece of trash on the floor, I pick it up. If something needs to be done because a team member is busy or has stepped away for a moment, I've been known to step in and help—not for accolades—simply because it is the right thing to do. I can learn as much from my team members as they can learn from me. We all have our own zone of genius to share with the world.

Don't Compare Yourself to Others

Confidence, self-esteem, and a drive for excellence and success, at the end of the day, come from within. Success is not because of willpower. It is a result of consistently striving, working hard, and learning. Asking for help from others is far easier with humility. Set your own micro-goals throughout the day, achieve them, and acknowledge your success. These habits help you build your self-confidence and self-reliance.

Don't Worry What Other People Think of You

Life is hard enough. It is filled with joy, triumphs, and more than enough challenges. Whenever you worry about what other people think of you, you are giving away your power, often stepping out of your zone of genius and draining your energy that can be spent in far better ways. Humility enables you to see yourself as you truly are, without a facade. Therefore, you don't need others' approval because you accept and embrace who you are without apologies.

Be Present in the Now

It is far easier to be present with others when I am not so focused on myself, my smartphone, or the last FB post or tweet I just read. Instead, I stand a far better chance of being present by consistently practicing this chapter's wisdom, which I learned from many who are much smarter than me. This commitment to being present is the secret behind the "magic first 5 minutes" I spend at the beginning of every patient appointment. I share specific details on how to conduct these magic 5 minutes in the chapters, *Did You Hear Me? Empathic Listening*; and *Achieving Service Excellence: Fostering a Culture of Quality Outcomes.*

Take Care of Yourself First

Flight attendants remind us on every flight, "Please place the oxygen mask over your own mouth and nose before assisting others." Without oxygen, we lose consciousness, and without our health, we risk losing everything.

Augusten Burroughs, author of *Running with Scissors,* wisely said, "When you have your health, you have everything. When you don't have your health, nothing else matters at all." Exercise, meditate, journal, pray, drink water, exercise your mind, and schedule appointments with yourself on your calendar. You will feel much better when you do, and you will have the energy to do what you love and help more people.

I Can Learn from Anyone

About ten years ago, I remember reading a quote from the famous college football coach, Lou Holtz that read,

> *Nothing* on this earth is *standing still.*
>
> It's either growing or it's dying.
>
> No matter if it's a tree or a human being.

I agree. I've been growing personally and professionally my entire life. I always feel the most alive when I'm learning something new. With my life-long learner mindset, I am genuinely interested, even intrigued, to learn from others. At 4M Institute*, our most successful students are dentists who similarly yearn to learn and are open to learning from experts who bring different paradigms and perspectives.

*The 4M Institute provides CE Credits and registers dentists who successfully complete courses at 4M Institute as credentialed members of the 4M Certified Dentists' Society. 4M Institute provides courses for everything from NeoArch to IV-Sedation, PFR/Phlebotomy, your assistants, sales and marketing for dentists, leadership, branding, and excellence in patient satisfaction.

No Fear of Failure

There's no shame in failing. To be good at anything, you must have experience. To gain experience, you get to make mistakes, and you can't make mistakes if you don't try. I've always seen failing as learning and learning as growth. Mistakes are an investment in my own journey to excellence. Wisdom and excellence are the fruits of confidently *doing,* not tentatively *trying.* You don't have to have it all figured out first. Instead, embrace the journey of discovery. Be scared and do it anyway!

I've had failures in business. I've lost property and lost some money along the way. I've learned so much from it. We learn so much more from our failures than our successes.

Yes, I threw my own pity party at the beginning, but soon after, I let the past be the past and looked forward. Then I kept moving, moving forward. There's no standing still.

Ten years ago, I was approached by a family friend to invest in their new concept for an energy drink. Along with another family member, we invested one million dollars in this company. Two years later, the company was dissolved. We lost our entire investment.

Lessons Learned

I learned I didn't want to be a silent partner ever again. Instead, when I invest in a company, I will have a managing role in the company. I trusted the product over the people. This is backward. I could have done far more due diligence on the people I was investing in. This made me a wiser investor, for sure.

"Get rich quick" doesn't exist, and don't fall for it. Now, when presented with one, I ask myself, "Why am I responding to "quick money?" I don't. I laugh and walk away. Even when you do get rich quickly, too often, it doesn't last. I learned not to trust anyone with my hard-earned money. More importantly, I learned the importance of valuing my hard-earned money—to respect and protect it.

For myself, I have always said,

> "I am competing with myself. Every day I want to become a better 'me' in some way."

This internal competition also bolsters my confidence and resilience in the face of failing to move forward. Sir Richard Branson, the billionaire founder of the Virgin Group, has written,

> "I suppose the secret to bouncing back is not only to be unafraid of failures but to use them as motivational and learning tools... There's nothing wrong with making mistakes if you don't make the same ones over and over again."

Power of Positivity

My experience has been rooted in the practical power of positivity. I believe each of us attracts the energy that we put out in the universe. We see this in our teams every day. When "superstar Nancy" comes in one day as "negative Nancy," we all feel it, and more importantly, we all experience it. Frankly, negativity, especially chronic negativity within an individual or a team, can kill your practice, driving away patients and team members.

Therefore, negativity is one of the more important attitudes we screen for in our hiring process, and during the first 30 days of onboarding our new hires. We have found team members with the trifecta of negativity, scarcity thinking, and a victim mindset do not last long. Frequently, the person quits on their own when they realize our teams do not embrace negativity, scarcity thinking, or a victim mindset.

Your Own Definition of Success

We all have our own definitions and measures of success. Our own expectations too. Our definition of success may change over time, based on wisdom from our experiences and lessons learned. Throughout this book, you will have the opportunity to explore your own definition of success from many angles, both personally and professionally.

You will discover, or rediscover, your definition for success for yourself, your people, your patients, and your practice. Tools, checklists, and self-assessments are available online on the resource page listed at the end of each chapter.

At the end of every chapter, you will also see two opportunities—Reflection and Action.

I invite you to pause at the end of each chapter and reflect on the quotes, questions, or thoughts in ***REFLECTION***. Self-awareness is essential and is a cornerstone of personal growth.

Taking action is the first step in integrating what you learn. After reflecting, I invite you to jot down your immediate thoughts after reading the ***ACTION*** section. Then schedule time on your calendar each week to revisit your notes from one chapter's ***REFLECTION*** and ***ACTION*** sections.

Scan the QR Code Below to hear Dr. Sean's
Personal Message Recap of this Chapter.

Chapter 1
REFLECTION:
Building Blocks for Personal Success

"If I want to make it, be successful, and make a big difference in this world, ***there's no standing still.****"*
—Dr. Sean

Self-awareness, the conscious knowledge of one's character, feelings, motives, and desires are key to your success as a leader and an entrepreneur.

Reflect on each of these on the list below:

1. Which of these are my natural strengths? Consider these in the context of your personal and professional life.

    - Humility
    - Hard Work and Hustle
    - Generosity/Giving
    - Ego vs. I Can Learn from Anyone
    - Not Comparing Self to Others/Not Worrying What Others Think of You
    - Being Present
    - Taking Care of Yourself First
    - Staying Calm in the Face of Change, Uncertainty, or Challenges
    - Emotional Intelligence – the capacity to be aware of, control, and express one's emotions and to handle interpersonal relationships judiciously and empathetically.
    - Managerial Courage – tactfully dispenses direct and actionable feedback; is open and direct with others

without being intimidating; deals head-on with people problems and prickly situations.

2. Which are strengths I learned and honed over time? Which present challenges or opportunities for my self-improvement?

3. What other values, beliefs, or principles guide me in my journey?

4. Do my team leaders and team members know my values, beliefs, or principles related to me, my role as owner/leader, and my expectations of others?

Chapter 1

ACTION:

Building Blocks for Personal Success

1. In addition to the ones listed above, list your values, beliefs, or principles. (Again, do your team leaders and members know these are important to you and your practice?)

2. Which principle, belief, or value deserves more attention now? Identify one specific commitment you will address over the next two weeks. What specific actions will you take to improve yourself? Communicate the importance of this to your team leaders and members.

3. Ask your team members, who know you or work with you the most, what they see as your strengths and opportunities for improvement in the specific areas of your choice.

"Everything changes, and nothing stands still."
—Heraclitus, pre-Socratic Greek philosopher

The following tools are available here:
www.TheresNoStandingStill.com

The Quality of Life 100 Self-Assessment
10 Steps to a Strong Personal Foundation
Energy Drains Exercise

CHAPTER 2

Striving for Excellence: Unleash Your Full Potential

"Whatever you do, do it well.
Do it so well that when people see you do it,
they will want to come back and see you do it again,
and they will want to bring others and show them
how well you do what you do."
—Walt Disney

My father was a no-nonsense kind of guy who never coddled me or my three brothers. Instead, he taught us the value of hard work and personal responsibility. At the age of nine, I worked hard at his print shop to earn my first bicycle. However, just two days after my father gave me my first bicycle, I carelessly left it unlocked outside a store, and it was stolen. Devastated, I waited two years before my father bought me another one. Lessons like this have served me my entire life by teaching me the importance of self-discipline and self-awareness.

Today, I demand excellence from myself and my team members to provide our patients with the best possible experience and results. Pursuing excellence has been a lifelong journey for me, and I strive to be better each day. For me, it's not about measuring myself against others but against my past performance. Whether I'm working to improve my speed and quality or transform a patient's life, I am driven by the pursuit of excellence.

The challenge for us dentists is spending so much time every day pursuing excellence by "doing the work" ourselves—being self-disciplined, self-driven, and self-reliant. As practice owners, we must remember not everyone on our team shares the same level of self-discipline, self-reliance, and commitment to excellence. To grow our people and our practice, we must share our expectations and provide guidance and support where needed.

Ways to Instill the Pursuit of Excellence

Discover the best practices for inspiring, engaging, and equipping your team members to pursue excellence with self-discipline and self-reliance. Spend 5-10 minutes with each team member as often as possible to build trust and show you genuinely care. Ask for their input, suggestions, and recommendations. Consistently communicate and celebrate excellent outcomes, no matter how big or small. It's one thing for you and me to do this ourselves, but are your practice managers and other leaders also doing this?

This book offers proven ways to solicit feedback and input from your team members.

Ensure all team members understand why pursuing excellence is vital for patients and the team. Conduct focus group discussions with patients, share the results with your team, and ask for improvement suggestions. Ask team members, "If you could change one thing to improve XYZ, what would it be?"

Excellence begins with us, and our team members are watching and listening to us every day. Model the pursuit of excellence and empower your team, avoiding micromanagement. Acknowledge feedback, engage in discussions, and follow up frequently. Challenge and engage team members, adding value to their work and contributions.

Team members who do not step up or re-engage will make a discovery at their own pace or be expedited by you and/or your practice manager. They will discover they have a choice, a decision to make-remain stagnant (at risk of losing their job), embrace change and growth, or leave on their own. The commitment we get to make is what training and support we are willing to invest in them.

You and I have invested significant sums of money, time, and energy to become excellent dentists and build our practices to transform our patients' lives. We know excellence is achieved together, with our teams; frankly, without them, there is no dental practice. Yet, that which is common sense is not always common practice. Therefore, as you think about excellence and discipline in yourself and your teams, I invite you to consider this:

Knowing you will be practicing dentistry for the next 10, 15, 25, or 35 more years, and many of your employees will be with you this entire time, the question is...

"How do you want to spend your remaining years as a dentist, a practice owner, a leader, and as a human being?"

Will you build something unique to patients and team members or just focus on the transactional day-to-day work? Turnover, attitudes, and morale reflect leadership and practice success. Invest in building something unique and high-quality and achieve success on your own terms.

The great news is your peers who have invested in building exceptionally high-quality practices are reaping the rewards financially, personally, and professionally. Some now own multiple practices, are acquiring or building more, and will ultimately benefit when they sell their practices. Some peers may achieve this before the age of 55. Are you on track with your own definition of success?

The pursuit of excellence makes a difference…

"My singing voice is even better after the procedure!"
—Didi Thomas

"As a former actress and singer in my 20s, I chose to get veneers. For decades I have endured a history of poor-quality dental work, resulting in rotting teeth, a second set of veneers, and later, six implants on my top and bottom arches.

At the age of 63, now a Clergy Rabbi, singing remains a vital part of my life. When I learned I needed a third round of veneers, I was hesitant. I was scheduled for a dental practice five minutes from my home. However, fate intervened when I contracted Covid and had to postpone the procedure.

During my recovery, television ads introduced me to 4M and the renowned Dr. Sean. Experiencing the exceptional quality of the entire team, I entrusted them with my dental journey. Despite the complexity of my case, with numerous implants and a problematic bridge, Dr. Sean and Dr. Athena guided me every step of the way.

The roof of my mouth plays a crucial role in my vocal abilities. I had concerns about its impact on my singing voice. However, after the All on 4 procedure, my singing voice is even better than before because they were so meticulous with the roof of my mouth, and my teeth are amazing. I tell everyone, "Don't go anywhere else, even if it requires a long drive to get there, it's well worth it!" This transformational experience left me speechless and singing with joy."

Beyond Our Practices

I invite you to consider the following:

- Beyond your dental practice, in what ways would you like to make a more significant impact?
- What are your visions of excellence for yourself, your practice, and your life?
- Beyond money, beyond the time freedom you have as a dentist (compared to other medical specialties), beyond doing quality work, and beyond taking care of patients, what is your vision for your life over the next 10 to 35 years as you practice dentistry, support your people, and better the lives of your patients?

Scan the QR Code Below to hear Dr. Sean's Personal Message Recap of this Chapter.

Chapter 2
REFLECTION:
Striving for Excellence

"The key to accepting responsibility for your life is to accept the fact that your choices, every one of them, are leading you inexorably to either success or failure, however you define those terms."
—Neal Boortz, author, radio show host

I invite you to ask yourself these questions and write down your responses.

1. What are the definitions of excellence and failure I have lived by so far?

2. Who instilled this in me--my parents, a mentor, a peer, or a professor?

3. If my team members, even my Associate Dentists or Partners, were asked what my definition of excellence is, how many of them would say the same thing, i.e., my definition of excellence?

4. When was the last time I shared with my entire team...
   a. ...my definition of excellence?
   b. ...the importance of our never-ending pursuit of excellence?
   c. ...why do these matter to me, for them, and especially for our patients?

5. What are some examples of the pursuit of excellence and discipline I can share with my team members?

For example, the way…

- ✓ we speak to our patients
- ✓ we communicate and collaborate as team members
- ✓ we show up to work every day (attitude, mindset, temperament)
- ✓ we handle inventory and supplies
- ✓ we keep our workstations organized, orderly, and neat
- ✓ we communicate with new patients when onboarding them
- ✓ we communicate with patients before, during, after visits, and procedures
- ✓ I succeeded and failed in different ways throughout my own life (vulnerability is key to building trust and credibility with your team members)

Perhaps set a reminder in your calendar for 6 months from today, so you can revisit these questions and see what progress you have made.

Chapter 2
ACTION:
Striving for Excellence

1. Ask your team to identify specific examples of behaviors, practices, systems, or methods from their work areas that contribute to excellence. Ask them, "*If you could change any one thing about our efforts and the way we deliver excellence, what would you change?*" Or, you may prefer asking them, "*What do we need to stop doing, start doing, and continue doing to improve in every area of our practice?*"

2. Review the feedback your team provides you. Respond to your team within seven days with what you heard, what you will support, and what you wish to implement immediately over the next 30-60 days and more long-term. Enroll an individual from each practice area to champion the specific improvement their team can implement. Engage your Quality Improvement Team or create one if you have not already.

3. Challenge each practice area to focus on consistently changing 1 or 2 habits to make progress on a specific improvement for 30 days. Your practice manager can check in weekly or bi-weekly with your Quality Improvement Team or your champions. Be sure to acknowledge a team member or team whenever you witness them making progress. Share patient feedback with your team that you and your practice manager are receiving.

The goal for you and your team, in the service of your patients, is to create quick wins, consistently improve, and build a culture of excellence within your entire practice. Every team is different; some may need more time to reach this goal. Focus on steadily developing your team by encouraging them to achieve simple, consistent improvements.

The following tools are available here:
www.TheresNoStandingStill.com

Stop, Start, Continue Feedback Exercise
Co-creating Behavior Standards Checklist
How to Build a High-Performance Culture Checklist

CHAPTER 3

The Wheel of Life: Balancing the Important Areas of Your Life

"What are the five things that will make my life go smoothly?"
—Dr. Sean Mohtashami

As a young dentist practicing in Las Vegas, I found early success and financial stability. I was in good health and physically fit. I spent a lot of time with our kids, my wife, and my extended family. Mentally and emotionally, things were great. I was reading lots of books back then.

But as my practice grew over the first ten years, I became too focused on money and building my post-graduate clinical skills that I neglected other important areas of my life, leading to a divorce and then missed opportunities with our three daughters. My ex-wife is a dentist as well. Luckily, we have built and maintained close, healthy, loving relationships with our daughters while effectively co-parenting. While I paid dearly for my choices at that time, the life lessons I learned were invaluable.

In 2007, a personal development course introduced me to the concept of the *Wheel of Life,* which helped me identify the eight domains of my life and where I needed to improve. I realized how many of these I had ignored, rationalized as not important at the time, or was simply blind to, consciously or unconsciously. Through daily reflection and seeking input from trusted peers, I was able to clarify what was most important to me and make changes for the better.

Now, when I'm living my best life, I prioritize my health, relationships, personal and professional development, career, and finances, while still finding joy and freedom in my journey. Finding fulfillment has been a lifelong pursuit. Hopefully, you may learn from my mistakes and take a closer look at your own *Wheel of Life* to live a meaningful, productive life on purpose.

The *Wheel of Life* Process

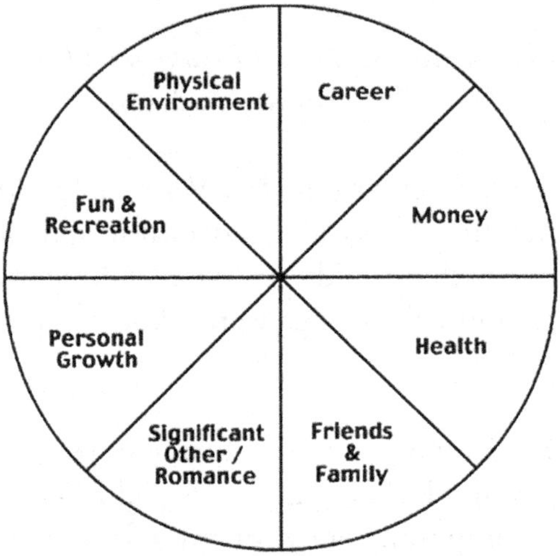

After completing the personal development course, working with the *Wheel of Life* the course had provided me, I began asking myself, "What are the most important things for me in my life?" As I made my list, I would check in with trusted peers, coaches, and close friends for their perspectives on living a meaningful, productive life on purpose.

I began to take time in my morning meditation to reflect on what was going well in my life, personally and professionally, and to ask myself more questions.

- In which areas of the *Wheel of Life* do I lack and need to improve personally and/or professionally?

- What results will be different a year from now after continuing what is working well, while also improving in other areas?

- How will my relationships improve?

I made a list of names of people in all aspects of my life. I took time to reflect on each relationship. Which ones are serving me? Which ones are not? Who have I neglected? Who deserves more of my personal time? From whom can I learn? To whom do I need to reach out? I made a concerted effort to let these people know how grateful I am for them, and to spend time or at least connect with them consistently.

After relationships, I began looking at every aspect of my life. Over the next few weeks, spending time on daily reflection, I began to clarify what was most important to me, and what changes I needed to make. I realized how each of these areas in my life are intertwined and interdependent.

I had taken my *eye off the ball* of what matters most, and now was my chance to commit to living the life I knew I deserved.

Focus on "The Big 5"

I decided to narrow down my wheel to focus on five areas of my life, which, when done well, significantly impact my results, experiences, and relationships.

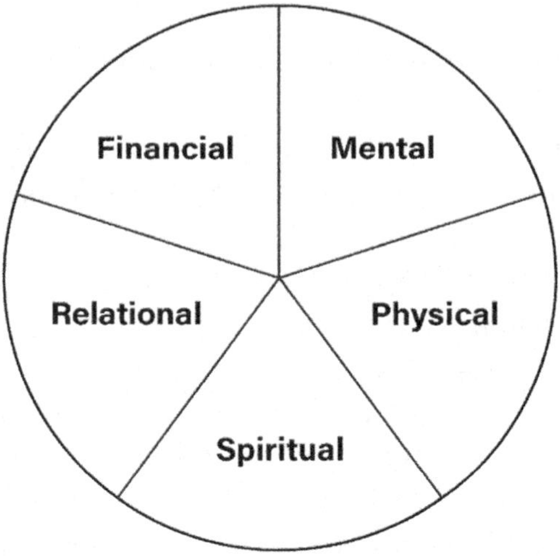

These are the five areas of focus that enable me to make the most significant impact on the eight domains of my *Wheel of Life*:

Mental: mental and emotional health; staying up-to-date and knowledgeable, learning, and growing (clinically and non-clinically)

Physical: keeping my physical body healthy; managing my physical environment

Financial: until your money is handled, you are not at choice in life

Spiritual: the feeling, sense, or belief that there is something greater than me, something more to being human than sensory experience, and the greater whole is cosmic or divine in nature

Relational: state of being connected with others—family, friends, acquaintances, romantic, professional, group/community; maintaining 5 relationship boundaries (physical, emotional, sexual, intellectual, financial); compassionate love

I invite you to step away from the *busyness and turmoil* of daily life and spend some personal time to reflect on what is working well and what needs your attention in terms of these five areas of your life—mental, physical, financial, spiritual, and relational.

After you have examined each area and determined your short list of priorities to address and improve, choose one area upon which to focus for 21 to 30 days. Then identify one specific action you will begin taking consistently to improve in this focus area.

Along my journey over the past 20 years, I have learned "work-life balance" is a myth. Instead, I make daily choices that move me closer to my goals of living a full, meaningful, productive, healthy life. The results of my choices sometimes take time to manifest, sometimes even decades. I've learned that being crystal clear about my goals, intentions, actions, and choices is critically important for myself and my impact on others.

Over the years, when I am focused on what matters most to me – the five things that make my life go smoothly – and I embrace my human needs, my life experiences are more rewarding. My results are more impactful.

When I do this well, others tell me they experience me as more grounded, humble, focused, passionate, and "on mission." I also have more energy and endurance and feel more confident and resilient to take on the day. Not easy, sure, but well worth the focus, energy, and discipline to do it.

Practical Steps for Taking Action

"Easier said than done," you may be thinking.

I acknowledge our lives get busy, complex, and, too often, overwhelming. We all struggle with unexpected challenges. I've experienced my own struggles, including investment losses, bad real estate deals, failed businesses, and difficult partnerships, to name a few. You have your own journey as well.

As we go through different seasons of life, our focus may change. Yet it's so important to revisit what matters most and work towards our goals. Here are some practices that have helped me over the years and could benefit you as well. Consider incorporating one of these into your daily routine:

- Practice guided meditation
- Write in a journal for five minutes each day
- Engage in different types of breathing techniques, such as diaphragmatic, mindful, deep, box/444, lion, or 478
- Experiment with Yoga, Tai Chi, Qigong, or other martial arts
- Get moving through walking, running, swimming, or calisthenics
- Incorporate prayer, or connect with nature
- Expand your knowledge by exploring various religious or spiritual experiences

Change can be intimidating, but taking small steps can lead to big transformations. Prioritizing your well-being is a journey worth taking.

Resolving Overwhelm

In the face of overwhelm, I have found "fast writing" helpful in many ways. Set aside five minutes of private time away from everyone else. Get creative. Sitting in your car in a parking lot works. Take out a piece of paper and a pen. Begin writing down all the thoughts, ideas, concerns, worries, and to-do items racing through your mind.

You are writing down everything in a "stream of consciousness" way without judgment, without thinking about it. Just write down the words as they come to you. Do not lift your pen from the paper. Keep writing. Let it flow out of you. Keep writing until you have nothing else coming to mind. Then and only then, stop and put down your pen.

Then close your eyes and take a few deep breaths. Focus on resting, releasing, or emptying your mind, whichever works best for you. Do not underestimate the power of this short, simple exercise. This is the first step in acknowledging your feelings and thoughts of overwhelm. You can expect to feel some form of release or relief. If nothing else, it helps quiet your mind. Later you can read the list, prioritize it, make a new to-do list, or do nothing with it, whatever works best for you.

Our Human Needs

Another valuable personal reflection opportunity, in support of crafting your own **Wheel of Life**, is to reacquaint yourself with your human needs. For millennia humankind has pursued a deeper understanding of what drives/motivates our human behavior and decision-making.

Throughout our lives, many times a day, every day, we either get our needs met or we don't. Honing your self-awareness of these human needs is profoundly useful when crafting your own definitions of excellence and success, your *Wheel of Life*, and your morning routine.

Just as the *Wheel of Life* helps you discover in which area of life you have been struggling or thriving (or avoiding), you may discover which of these human needs are not being met in your personal and professional lives.

Tony Robbins' definitions of our human needs are:

- **Certainty**: assurance you can avoid pain and gain pleasure
- **Uncertainty/Variety**: the need for the unknown, change, and new stimuli
- **Significance**: feeling unique, important, special, or needed
- **Connection/Love**: a strong feeling of closeness or union with someone/something
- **Growth**: an expansion of capacity, capability, or understanding
- **Contribution**: a sense of service, focus on helping, giving to, and supporting others

Robbins has taught for decades that these core needs drive all decisions which humans make.

We've all heard the statistics about the amount of stress we dentists endure and the grave risk we have for depression, anxiety, burnout, and suicidal ideation as a result. Due to this chronic stress, we are at risk of succumbing to a host of other maladies, and the most devastating is the tragic loss of life.

You and I live this every day. We intellectually know it. We feel its impact. Too often, we rationalize it for myriad reasons. Burnout is real. Too many of us suffer silently, holding on to our secret, hoping no one will find out. Yet many of us are exhausted from the journey. The good news: there are ways to address, navigate, resolve, and overcome burnout. There are proven ways to reduce the risk of burnout. There are ways to thrive.

In reading the next chapter, *Bouncing Back from Burnout: Rebuilding Resilience*, you may see yourself and your specific risks or causes of burnout, possibly for the first time.

Scan the QR Code Below to hear Dr. Sean's
Personal Message Recap of this Chapter.

Chapter 3
REFLECTION:
The Wheel of Life

1. What are the most important things for me in my life?

2. What are the five things that will make my life go smoothly?

3. In which areas of my Wheel of Life do I lack, and do I need to improve personally and/or professionally?

4. What results will be different a year from now if I keep doing what is working well while also improving in other areas?

5. Which of the six human needs are being met in my life right now? Which human need would benefit from more of my attention?

6. How will my relationships improve?

7. What am I avoiding?

Chapter 3
ACTION: The Wheel of Life

1. Give yourself the gift of doing a "**Fast Writing**" exercise to unload your thoughts onto a piece of paper. Follow the suggested steps in this chapter.

2. Complete your own ***Wheel of Life Personal Map***.

3. Invite one or two people who know you well to talk privately about your ***Wheel of Life***.

4. Review our human needs checklist and identify which human needs are currently being met for you and which are not.

5. Select one of the human needs to work on over the next 30 days as a form of self-care. Determine what you get to stop doing, start doing, and continue doing to improve your life.

The following tools are available here:
www.TheresNoStandingStill.com

The Wheel of Life Personal Map
Our Human Needs Checklist

CHAPTER 4

Bouncing Back from Burnout: Rebuilding Resilience

*"**Burnout** is a syndrome conceptualized as resulting from chronic workplace stress that has not been successfully managed."*
International Classification of Diseases
WHO, January 2022

Burnout for Dentists

The overarching categories of burnout for dentists are emotional exhaustion, depersonalization, and reduced personal accomplishment.

Emotional exhaustion refers to clinicians feeling emotionally, physically, and spiritually drained from chronic workplace stress and overwork.

Depersonalization refers to dentists becoming numb, callous, negative, cynical, or detached from their work.

Reduced personal accomplishment is defined as the tendency to negatively evaluate the worth of one's work, feeling insufficient to perform one's job, experiencing reduced professional efficacy, and poor professional self-esteem. I have done this myself when I think about being "Just an overpaid technician." This belief is inaccurate and dismisses the true value of what I do every day to change lives and save lives.

Every dentist has their own personality traits, goals, dreams, aspirations, and challenges. As a result, there is no magic pill or secret solution for "all dentists;" however, there are tactics and strategies to minimize the risk of burn-out or possibly overcome and resolve burn-out. Again, this is easier said than done, yet worth the effort to explore solutions, especially from our peers who have gone before us.

Once you have identified your specific symptoms and stressors, taking action toward solutions is paramount. The following is not a prescription but rather information and best practices to raise your self-awareness and help you identify actions that can be taken or practiced over time to mitigate burnout.

Burnout Symptoms

According to various studies globally, the following are the ten most common symptoms of burnout for dentists. Take note of which ones resonate for you.

- ✓ Emotional exhaustion
- ✓ Nagging, lingering frustrations
- ✓ Feeling completely spent at the end of the day
- ✓ Waking up late or not looking forward to another day at the office
- ✓ Chronic fatigue
- ✓ Sporadic mealtime, even skipping meals
- ✓ Less energized, motivated, or inspired by your work—loss of interest
- ✓ Feeling withdrawn, desensitized, or detached from your work and people
- ✓ Questioning yourself, lack of feeling competent
- ✓ Anxiety or racing thoughts

Research has identified 21 burnout symptoms most commonly experienced by dentists. I have experienced at least nine or more of these myself over the years. They seem to come in waves at different points in life.

Our lives seem to have seasons over the years. Growth in the spring, the flourishing, blooming, and bearing fruit of summer, and the beautiful slumbering of the fall. As Donna Long poignantly shared in *The Earth is Good*, "Nature in winter is a time of struggle and beauty. Winter signals the end of a long productive year." Our opportunity is to acknowledge our symptoms and the season we are experiencing.

Stressors Linked to Burnout

Dentists are under constant time pressure as they attempt to provide quality treatment for their patients within the allotted time frame, with little or no breaks from the high-pressure work environment. This can lead to feeling overwhelmed and anxious about whether they can deliver the expected level of care. Dentists must endure long hours requiring high levels of concentration. This can be taxing on their mental and physical health, with feelings of exhaustion leading to fatigue and an overall decrease in job performance.

Doing the same thing repeatedly on a daily basis can lead to a sense of monotony, contributing to burnout. Financial pressures, such as loans, mortgages, cash flow, receivables, and insurances can be intimidating for dentists. Unresolved conflicts, such as difficulties working with associates, team members, vendors/suppliers, and patients, can be a significant source of stress.

Self-criticism and recurring thoughts of mistakes, doubts, and expectations can lead to feelings of inadequacy or insecurity. Dentists may have recurring thoughts or doubts about their ability to provide the highest standards of patient care or whether they are up to date on the latest advancements in dentistry. Having unrealistic expectations, self-imposed or imposed by others, for their own performance as business owner, leader, and dentist, can also create high levels of stress.

Some of the most significant stressors linked to burnout are institutional or systems-based issues, yet many of them are personal belief and mindset challenges and leadership opportunities.

- ✓ Which stressors are negatively impacting you the most right now?
- ✓ Which stressors do you have control over or the ability to change?
- ✓ Which one of the leadership opportunities do you get to address (unresolved conflicts, lack of delegation, managing financial pressures)?
- ✓ What specifically happens if you don't address any of these stressors for 30 more days?

At the end of this chapter, you will see how to access the ***Burnout Symptoms and Stressors Checklist*** which covers the twenty-one burnout symptoms most commonly experienced by dentists, and more detail on the thirteen stressors linked to burnout.

Quick Tip

Implementing or optimizing block scheduling is one proven tactic to address the challenge of constant time pressure immediately. Block scheduling makes scheduling more efficient and productive, helping you achieve your production goals and providing excellent patient care. You can better protect your own schedule as well. Larger practices tend to use block scheduling, with color-coding by appointment value, so the scheduler can assist in maximizing production value. It's also easier to schedule patients based on the purpose of their visit.

Too often, I hear from peers who have let scarcity thinking or financial pressure (real or imagined) dictate their schedule. In dental school, many students dream of the time freedom they will have by owning their own practice. Unfortunately, dentists often build a job for themselves, not a business. I did this myself for the first three years after dental school. This issue also impacts one of the other big stressors, feeling a lack of control.

Strategies to Minimize Burnout

More dental schools are adapting their curriculum to address the most pressing needs of dentists today. After reviewing the latest research and publications in the dental industry and the progress being made in dental schools, there are some common themes related to burnout for dental schools and dental practices.

Undergraduate programs and graduate dental schools are beginning to provide more professional development opportunities in the domains of leadership, communication, business management, finance, and stress management skills, including suicide prevention.

Beyond the strategies shared in this chapter, you will find helpful tools, tactics, and techniques that help mitigate burnout in the other sections of this book, *YOUR PEOPLE, YOUR PATIENTS*, YOUR PRACTICE, and the online resources available.

Next is a list of actions to consider taking, organized by Leadership, Self-care, and Mindset domains. The various coaches I have worked with over the years have helped me see the importance of these three domains and how they impact every aspect of my life, personally and professionally. These proven tactics may be some of the most valuable tools you receive from this book.

LEADERSHIP

Get Clear About the Cause

In addition to your own reflection and efforts to identify the root cause of your burnout or impending burnout, I encourage you to ask for feedback from your business partners, associates, peers, mentors, coaches, advisors, or spouse/partner. Most importantly, ask those who observe or experience you in various situations or at least spend enough time with you for their feedback to be constructive or instructive. Getting clear for yourself, based on others' feedback, not just your own perspective, is helpful.

Deep Dive on Expectations

Due to many factors, not the least of which is personality traits, it is common for dentists to struggle with self-imposed stress from their own unrealistic expectations or perfectionism. There may be expectations of themselves, their personal and professional goals, the targets for their practice, and financial goals. An executive or business coach may help you explore how realistic, achievable, timely, and even rational your goals and expectations are. Far too often, dentists are "their harshest critics."

Reframe Bad News

When communicating bad news or necessary yet difficult news to your team members or patients, strive to avoid the common mistake of misplaced responsibility, i.e., thinking or worrying about what they will think about you when they hear the news. Many dentists relate to having perfectionist tendencies and/or being "people pleasers."

Understandably, delivering bad news is not easy for these dentists. Reframing the situation to something like, "This situation, condition, or result does not define me, nor put me in a negative light…it happened, and it is what it is. It is my responsibility to communicate this with my team or patient." Also, reframing the act of delivering bad news as "This is a great way to support my team members and help them by telling them."

Reframe Conflict

Avoiding difficult conversations with people, whether team members or patients, does nothing to resolve the situation. Again, many people avoid conflict for a variety of reasons, especially due to concerns over the impact on the relationship with the other person. Instead of seeing difficult conversations as a negative, or catastrophizing the potential outcome, simply reframe it. Instead, go to the person with whom you are having a difficult conversation with your intention being, "I care enough about you to tell you."

Address Unresolved Office Issues

Letting office issues fester is a management, leadership, and business failure. Like dealing with difficult conversations/interpersonal conflict, with unresolved office issues, everyone is watching you to see when you will handle this office issue. Dentists who are poor managers/leaders fail and lose the respect of their team members every time they avoid and delay addressing these issues. In other sections of this book and online resources, tools, tactics, and scripted language (key-words) help you navigate these situations.

SELF-CARE

Minimize Isolation

Dentists understandably may find themselves in a daily routine that keeps them feeling stuck, and like they have no life outside of work. Several of the stressors for dentists are working long hours under constant time pressure, with long spans requiring high levels of concentration; repeatedly performing the same procedures; working in small spaces; dealing with financial pressures; "calling the shots" all day as an owner and suffering chronic fatigue.

Find ways to schedule time with others outside of work and beyond your family members. Join a book club, volunteer at a shelter, play golf with a different foursome or walk your dog with a neighborhood friend. Reaching out to engage with others brings new life, experiences, joy, and connections. Chronic isolation is a recipe for disaster long term.

Ask for Help

For many reasons, dentists tend to "suffer silently" rather than ask for help from others, especially men. If you struggle with asking for help, reframe it this way. "What need is being met by continuing to suffer on my own?" Or "What is possible when I simply __________."

Another question, based on brain science work, you can ask yourself is, "If I could change any one thing immediately, what would I change?" When asking yourself this question, there are no limits on resources to achieve what you say in response. Or ask yourself the classic Dr. Phil question, "How's that working for you?"

My life changed in so many great ways over the years whenever I silenced my ego and asked for help from coaches, advisors, mentors, peers, and friends. I hired a fitness coach to work out with me. I hired him, so I am accountable to someone else every morning to get out of bed and work out. He has helped me achieve my health and fitness goals because he keeps showing up every morning.

Form Your Own Mastermind Group

Over the years, I kept hearing about "mastermind groups," yet I wouldn't join one. Then, with my business coach's help, I saw the light and brought together my dream team of peers, mentors, advisors, and entrepreneur friends. This is another excellent way to minimize isolation. There's an old saying among CEOs, "It's lonely at the top."

This is true for us as well. Everyone on our team looks to us for answers, instructions, encouragement, feedback, and coaching. But who do you have in your life with whom you can confide your personal and professional challenges, bounce ideas off, or ask questions?

You can start small with three or four members of your own mastermind group. When you meet, you can each ask the group a question about life or business and then sit back and receive their input, suggestions, and feedback. Doing this once a month can be so valuable, personally and professionally. Make a list of your "dream team" to invite to your mastermind group. Then invite them to hop on a Zoom call once a month.

Pick a Passion Project

This one is different from the suggestions under "Minimize Isolation." This is about doing something you want to do, which may or may not involve other people. So many dentists tell me how they sold their golf clubs when they had their second child, gave up tennis, never started painting or making pottery, or stopped working on their classic car sitting in their garage. Find a new passion project or reconnect with a former one. Discover new hobbies, learn a new skill, start collecting, read your 20 favorite books in a year, start antiquing, get a rescued golden retriever and teach her new tricks, or reconnect with your faith.

Variety is the Spice of Life

I might have never discovered implant dentistry if I hadn't been willing to learn new dental procedures. I could have kept practicing as a general dentist in that Las Vegas practice and perhaps retired from there. Instead, I embraced my inner voice—being a lifelong learner—and learned sedation dentistry. This truly changed my life.

It opened the door to a world of possible dental specialties I could pursue. I learned restorative and cosmetic dentistry, then one day

I discovered implant dentistry. I was hooked. I loved everything about implant dentistry. These graduate programs and additional certifications and licenses enabled me to provide more services for my patients. This variety of skills and procedures has afforded me a life in dentistry beyond my imagination.

The 4M Dental Implant Center and the 4M Institute exist today because I listened to my head and heart, asked for help from others, and believed in myself and what was possible. You can too. Create a "Dream 10 List" of what you would love to learn and practice and what you would love to achieve personally and professionally.

MINDSET OPPORTUNITIES

I shared some of my own mindset beliefs in the chapter, *Building Blocks for Personal Success*, and *Feedback Fuels Team Success.* Here I am sharing the most common mindset challenges and opportunities according to current research and surveys of dentists.

Again, we all have our unique combination of beliefs, values, principles, education, and experience. This list is meant to be a catalyst for you to think about your mindset, not a prescription for solutions.

Consider what's working well and what may no longer serve you.

Discover Your Behavioral Style and Unlock Stronger Relationships

Do you approach problems with a detail-oriented, analytical mindset? According to Tony Alessandra's Platinum Rule, this puts you squarely in the Thinker quadrant. While your eye for accuracy and persistence makes you an asset in many situations, it can also lead to analysis paralysis and an inability to see the big picture.

Understanding your behavioral style is crucial to effective communication with others. Three other styles exist: Relater, Director, and Socializer. Upwards of 65-70% of healthcare staff and nurses fall into the Relater category, valuing harmony and collaboration over conflict.

Recognizing and adapting to others' styles will lead to fewer misunderstandings, stronger work relationships, and increased leadership effectiveness. Ultimately, understanding your own style can help you identify and eliminate burnout-inducing behaviors like perfectionism and unrealistic expectations of yourself. Don't let your style isolate you from others. Learn more about yourself and those around you to become a more effective, empathetic leader.

The Value of Understanding Your Style

Understanding my own style helped me understand why I would get frustrated, even upset, with certain things people did or said in the office. It helped me realize that most people I interact with are not *Thinkers*, so I adapt my style to ensure they feel heard, understood, respected, and valued.

Understanding styles helps you minimize and sometimes eliminate some of the stressors of burnout. For *Thinkers*, understanding their behavioral style may help them understand their tendency toward perfectionism, being overly self-critical, skeptical, possibly becoming cynical, and having unrealistic expectations of themselves.

The Great Opportunity to Transform

We all have limiting beliefs and *stories* we tell ourselves about why our world is the way it is. Unfortunately, many of these beliefs and stories are distorted.

Some of the more common mindset issues for dentists, which are best addressed with the help of counselors, psychologists, or psychiatrists, are:

- ✓ **Needing to Be Liked**

- ✓ **People Pleasing**
- ✓ **Worrying What Others' Expectations Are of Them**
- ✓ **Perfectionism**
- ✓ **Unrealistic Expectations of Self**
- ✓ **Failing to Value Their Worth**
- ✓ **"My Identity is All About Being a Dentist"**

Can you relate to any of these? What are other beliefs or stories you tell yourself?

I've worked on three mindset beliefs in my own life: worrying about others' expectations of me, perfectionism, and unrealistic expectations of myself. These tendencies are born from fears that can hold me back from taking action and create anxiety about the future. They can also lead to procrastination and task avoidance.

My drive for excellence can fuel unrealistic expectations of myself, but it has also caused me to overextend and experience burnout. This has led me to make commitments to others that were difficult to fulfill and therefore created excessive work hours. However, I value my work ethic, commitment to excellence, and follow-through on commitments.

Here are some tips I've learned along the way:

- Take clear, precise, and appropriate action to overcome perfectionism, overwhelm, and anxiety.
- See situations and conditions as they are, no better, no worse, and address them head-on and quickly, which reduces stress and anxiety.
- Acknowledge mistakes and forgive yourself fully to stay on track with your daily demands.
- Resist the urge to judge yourself to harshly and instead, see everything as an opportunity to learn and improve.

> *You must never confuse faith that you will prevail in the end— which you can never afford to lose— with the discipline to confront the most brutal facts of your current reality, whatever they might be.*
>
> – **Admiral James Bond Stockdale,** US Navy, Vietnam War POW, Medal of Honor recipient

If you struggle with similar mental blocks, try incorporating these tips into your own personal growth journey. Ask for help. Find a coach. Find an accountability partner who is similarly committed to their own personal growth.

YOU AND I ARE NOT ALONE

Unfortunately, the risk of burnout is real for you and me every day. You may be struggling with it right now. You may know someone who is struggling with burnout, even severely right now.

I understand how powerful and challenging burnout can be in many aspects of our daily lives at work and at home. I have struggled with burnout myself in several ways over the years–divorce, failing business, losing investments, and struggling relationships.

If you are experiencing burnout, you are not alone.

I hope you will ask for help, so you don't suffer alone. Asking for help was not always easy for me, even though I was experiencing significant pain. Often, we avoid asking for help because of our pride, ego, or fears–e.g., fear of change, rejection, failure, shame, or loss.

The irony is that you and I, as dentists, have dedicated our lives to helping others, including our patients and our families, yet do we take care of ourselves?

Asking for help can be one of the greatest acts of self-care, courage, and strength you can demonstrate. I recommend reaching out to a trusted friend or family member, seeking professional help (e.g., therapy or counseling), joining support groups, or hiring a coach.

In writing this chapter, I hope to offer you the chance to practice self-care, so you can be the best version of yourself, with the energy and passion to serve others and love your loved ones. The good news is… there are more tools throughout this book and online to help you take specific steps toward personal growth and improvement. In fact, in the next chapter, Julieanne O'Connor, the Director of 4M Institute and a Quality-of-Life Coach, provides techniques to achieve success without sacrificing the quality of your life. You may especially enjoy the *Success Windows Reflection Exercise.*

988 Suicide and Crisis Lifeline

If you or someone you know, has a mental illness, is struggling emotionally, or has concerns about their mental health, call or text 988, to connect with a trained crisis counselor.
Or use **Lifeline Chat** on the web (English only) via https://988lifeline.org/chat/

The Lifeline provides 24-hour, confidential support to anyone in suicidal crisis or emotional distress.

Chapter 4
REFLECTION:
Bouncing Back from *Burnout*

Burnout Symptoms

1. Which burnout symptoms have you experienced in the past year?

2. Which burnout symptoms are you experiencing now?

3. Which burnout symptoms are you most concerned about right now?

Stressors Linked to Burnout

1. Which stressors are negatively impacting you the most right now? Which can you control?

2. What's the root cause of your stress right now?

3. Which one of the leadership opportunities, unresolved conflicts, or unaddressed office issues do you get to address first?

4. What happens if you don't address these stressors for 30 more days?

FYI:

Today research continues exploring which factor contributes the most to the high risk of burnout for dentists—environment, the dental care delivery system, or individual characteristics of dentists.

Chapter 4
ACTION:
Bouncing Back from Burnout

1. List your burnout symptoms and prioritize the top 2 to address immediately.

2. Prioritize the top 2 stressors you can control or influence to change that you want to address immediately.

3. Which strategy to minimize burnout will you begin to implement immediately? From which category... Leadership, Self-Care, or Mindset?

4. Who could you reach out to right now who may be struggling with burnout? Call them right now, or at least text or email them.

5. Launch Your Own Mastermind Group: Make your dream invitation list of those to invite to join your new mastermind group. Start to outline your stepwise plan to invite people to join your mastermind group and begin to reach out to them.

The following tools are available here:
www.TheresNoStandingStill.com

Burnout Symptoms and Stressors Checklist
Starting Your Own Private Mastermind Checklist

CHAPTER 5

Success and Your Quality of Life

"Success does not have to come at the expense of your quality of life."
—Julieanne O'Connor, Quality of Life Coach

Julieanne O'Connor is a great life coach who has helped me personally and professionally and is invaluable to the success of 4M Institute. I asked Julieanne to share her insights on the pursuit of success and its impact on quality of life.

Quality of Life

As a high achiever, I have experienced great success and grave failure in my personal and professional life. I have realized that these highs and lows are a part of life's journey, and more of them are inevitable. Embracing this reality has helped me approach these situations with more calm and less emotional reactions.

Reaching a peak in one's career can be a thrilling experience, but it is important to take a moment to appreciate the accomplishment and be grateful for it before moving on to the next goal. Successful people often encounter times of unhappiness and depression after reaching a peak, leading them to constantly strive for the next one without taking a break in between.

While it is natural to strive for success, we must remember that what goes up must come down. Based on the nature of the highest-highs and lowest-lows, one naturally encounters a diverse space "in between" in which to live. The secret to happiness falls in the "in between."

> The secret to happiness falls in the *in between.*

Reflection during this time can help us better understand our interpretation of life and achieve a more fulfilling existence.

There are many worthwhile questions to ask during a post-win reflective period. It can be especially beneficial to question your interpretation of life as it happens in the "in between."

I invite you to consider:

- ✓ Can satisfaction be found in the mundane?
- ✓ Can you give yourself and your team a place to breathe after a great win? If yes, for how long before the rat race happens again?
- ✓ Can you find simple pleasures in boredom?
- ✓ Can you be fully present with the people you are with at any given time, although you have other things going on?
- ✓ What is enough, and why do your accomplishments matter?
- ✓ How can you use what you've accomplished—along with your epic fails—to lay the groundwork for each new step to reach the next phase with more ease, more freedom, or more simplicity?
- ✓ How do you bring your life up until now into this present moment?

I was once asked by a highly driven and successful dental professional, "What happens if I learn to maintain complete satisfaction with where I'm at? Won't I lose my drive?"

I replied, "Do you ever maintain a sense of complete satisfaction?"

"No," he laughed, "I guess it's the human condition."

However, sustainable joy can be achieved by simply having curiosity about your life, its meaning, and embracing what unfolds. This, coupled with being okay with the mundane and personal growth, will stimulate your mind and create peace of mind. Personal growth is a valuable way to stretch capabilities and stimulate your mind. When you grow, you tend to improve areas of your life which are of interest. This can make your mind more imaginative and keep it active.

When you are in a growth mindset, it causes you to be more aware of changes taking place. Both awareness and change itself can be fulfilling. In addition, when you are growing, there is often more time spent conscious of present moment events which can create peace of mind. Plus, you will often increase your personal value which can clearly be rewarding.

Moreover, giving can benefit you in ways you might not have realized. Along with rewarding those who receive, research shows that giving stimulates the same areas of the brain that eating, or sex does. The act of giving creates rewards for both the giver and receiver. When you actively focus on living a fulfilling and rewarding life, you'll give meaning to your life.

Determine What Matters Most

One way to get grounded in a post-win or post-fail reflective period is to commit a little time to revisiting where you're at now; what you desire; and, most importantly, why.

This *Success Windows Reflection Exercise* can be done on a piece of paper or on a whiteboard to help you quickly gain clarity about what truly matters to you personally.

You can download the form,
Success Windows Reflection Exercise
www.TheresNoStandingStill.com.

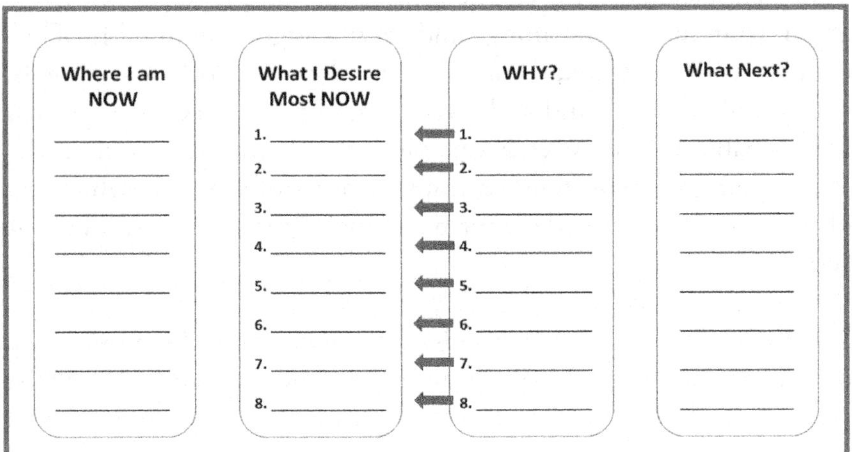

SUCCESS WINDOWS REFLECTION EXERCISE

In the first column, "Where I am NOW," jot down everything that comes to mind about where you are now. This can be in your career, relationships, and/or anything that comes to mind. Just as fast as you can think of it, put it down on paper. This is called "fast writing."

Next, think about what you most want or desire currently. In the second column, "What I Desire Most Now," "fast write" everything you dream you could have right now.

Then in the third column, "WHY," jot down your answers to the question, "Why?", to each of the items on the second column, "What I Desire Most Now." As you do this, try to drill down deeper into each answer as to why this answer is important to you personally.

Example: "I want to buy a new car."

1. Why? "Because I earned it."
2. Why? "Because it will give me a sense of luxury for all my hard work."
3. Why? "Because I want to feel relaxed."
4. Why? "Because when I feel relaxed, I tap into total peace of mind."

You may find after drilling down deep enough that you don't need a new car because it will cost you more, leading to more time at work and, ultimately, giving you *less* peace of mind. You may find what you really want is more leisure time which is better realized without the added debt or cost of a new car.

However, maybe you get clear that the luxury car *is* important because you spend enough time in it that it's worth the expense. Whatever the outcome, the idea is to get completely clear about *WHY* anything you desire truly matters so you don't inadvertently chase a desire that takes you further away from the important things that matter most to you.

Often by revisiting in deep reflection your WHY beneath what you want, you can find yourself eliminating things you may have initially thought were important or replacing some items with more meaningful priorities.

Building a strategy to reach your goals is the easy part. Once you're clear on where you're at, what you want, and WHY, you are more likely to take action in pursuit of what you desire.

Highs and Lows

A superb quality of life is dependent on a life lived moment-by-moment between the highs and lows.

Achieving a high-quality life includes experiencing both highs and lows, taking note of the sacrifices and benefits that accompany success. Goals have a place; and with each success there are varied degrees of sustainable highs, leaving in their path mostly only stories of what was. When determining what success looks like, your quality of life should always be checked against the benefits and sacrifices which are a part of the overall formula.

Alongside setting goals, determining your personal idea of fulfillment is essential. Striving for growth and being generous can lead to greater happiness, as can embracing curiosity and peace. Although success and failure both offer distinct advantages, when used positively, success can provide meaningful influence, while failure offers invaluable opportunities for introspection and improvement. By understanding what fulfillment means to you and making a roadmap, you can continually improve your life experience, regardless of the highs or lows you encounter.

Hard Work, Sacrifice, and Cost

Success and a strong work ethic often go hand in hand, but some achieve immense success at great personal cost. Those who have risen to great heights may lose sight of what's truly important–for example, Dr. Sean's journey with *The Wheel of Life*. The anticipation of reaching a goal can lead to a dopamine rush, but the feeling dissipates once the goal is achieved. This can lead to depression and a lack of motivation.

Take post-Olympic depression or post-win depression as examples. Even consider post-lottery winner depression. The "arrival fallacy" as termed by psychology expert/author Tal Ben-Shahar explains how dopamine is released during the anticipation of reaching a goal and how once it's achieved, the brain stops producing it at the prior levels. Understandably, over-achievers can succumb to the addiction of dopamine produced during phases of extreme activity.

It's important to take time to recover and appreciate the journey. When it comes to meeting goals, if you "under-recover," you basically spin your wheels, working very hard with no change in performance. It is critical to fully recover by taking time off from the constant fast pace, stress, and pressure of peak performance. Many peak performers fail to learn this.

Work-life balance isn't always feasible for high achievers, but remembering your purpose can help you balance your priorities. A coach, mentor, or accountability partner can help you stay focused and grounded in what matters most and your *why* behind what you are doing. As you navigate life, remember to adjust your priorities and stay true to your values. A coach can provide valuable guidance and support as you pursue success.

When I connect with my coach, I can openly share my thoughts and feelings, whether it's uncertainty, excitement, or boredom. Through insightful questions, my coach helps me gain clarity and empowers me to feel courageous and fulfilled. He maintains a focus on my values and who I want to be, challenging me to take action towards my goals. My coach continues to guide me and ensure I remain grounded in what truly matters.

Time

Time is irreplaceable, yet many people waste it on meaningless tasks. Evaluate how you spend your time and make sure it aligns with your personal goals and dreams. I grew up on a contaminated property outside of Reno, Nevada. I was told at a young age that I could get cancer from what I'd been exposed to on the land. Because of that experience, I learned early on that time is valuable, and I quickly decided I'd never let a single day go by without feeling grateful for my time.

I also decided to make it a mission to build meaningful relationships throughout my life. As I became deeply interested in relationships, asking everyone I met to tell me more about their lives, I became intensely curious about what created sustainable joy and a sense of a fulfilled life. Leveraging our time is the key.

By outsourcing and partnering strategically, you can buy back your most valuable resource and live a life of joy and purpose. Understanding what truly matters to you is the first step in getting the most out of your time.

The Choice Is Yours

Success comes in many different forms, each unique to the individual. Some work tirelessly, others struggle but persist, while some thrive on the excitement of the chase. Some move at lightning speed yet maintains a sense of calm. Within this diverse group, you'll find visionaries, technicians, educators, motivators, and dreamers, often a combination of these types. Some lead, mentor, and motivate, while others may use others as steppingstones. Some speed through life like a train and others like a raft slowly floating down stream. Still others combine both methods. There are those who are driven by fear and those who are driven by meaning. There are those who take and those who give.

The Question is...

> "Who Do You Choose to Become?"

Chapter 5

REFLECTION: Success and Your Quality of Life

1. Reflect on "The secret to happiness falls in the 'in between.'"

2. Can I find satisfaction in the mundane?

3. Can I be fully present with others while handling other things?

4. With whom could I be fully present during our next conversation?

5. Am I driven by fear or driven by meaning?

6. What is my purpose for working this hard?

7. Who do I choose to become?

Scan the QR Code with Your Smartphone
Or go to https://youtu.be/NoRP4Pc23JQ
For a special message about Quality of Life

Chapter 5

ACTION:
Success and Your Quality of Life

Complete the Success Window Reflection Exercise.

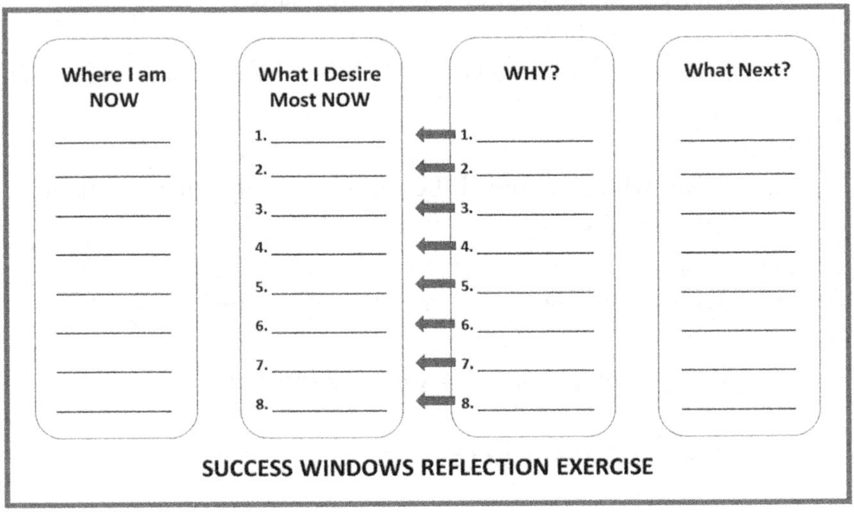

SUCCESS WINDOWS REFLECTION EXERCISE

The following tools are available here:
<u>www.TheresNoStandingStill.com</u>

<u>The Success Windows Reflection Exercise Worksheet</u>

CHAPTER 6

The Power of Influence: Making a Positive Impact in Your World

Having received invaluable coaching from Julieanne O'Connor and working with her since the inception of 4M Institute, I invited her to contribute her wisdom for this chapter.

"Ideas will lead to astonishing results when influence is integrated as a key part of any growth strategy."
—Julieanne O'Connor

Influence can be a powerful tool in achieving your objectives quickly and efficiently. For dental practices, it can help grow your brand and foster a positive culture. On the other hand, the cost of not leveraging your influence can lead to mistakes, wasted time and energy, and duplication of efforts.

By becoming an influencer within your industry, you can open doors to new opportunities, resources, creativity, and collaborations with others. Imagine having the ability to ask individuals or groups to contribute their resources and networks to your mission. Picture reaching a level of influence that inspires a multitude of people to align with you towards a common goal.

Dr. Sean has learned the power of influence throughout his career. By committing to learning foundational psychological principles and surrounding himself with highly influential people, Dr. Sean has become a strong and effective leader.

There are seven fundamentals of influence that you can use to grow your impact and results. By following these fundamentals, you can maximize your influence, increase patient retention, and build a strong and cohesive team.

7 Fundamentals of Influence

1. Identify your ideal audience and what sets you apart.
2. Understand your team's or patient fears and desires.
3. Stand out and connect.
4. Build credibility and trust.
5. Enroll people in your vision and mission–reinforce and reward.
6. Take responsibility.
7. Collaborate with others.

1. Identify Your Ideal Audience and What Sets You Apart

To leverage your influence, you must first understand your ideal audience and what sets you apart from the competition. Ask yourself who you love working with or serving and what type of patient or employee fits well within your organization's culture. Additionally, identify what sets your practice apart and why patients love your practice and refer others.

Some examples of *What Might Set You Apart* could be:

Doctor

- The doctor is a published author, board certified, leading expert.
- The doctor invented a patented process or device.
- The doctor started a foundation and/or an institute for their specialty.
- The doctor honors and celebrates certain cultural traditions with patients.

Practice

- Pain-free sedation dentistry with an anxiety-conscious staff who counsel patients from start to finish (anxiety-elimination concierge).
- Specialization of services known as the leading expert in their single specific service (it is okay to offer other services, yet focus is on a single service).
- Mobile pop-up dental clinics are provided pro bono.

Patient Experience

- On-site personal boutique: massage, facials, Botox, acupuncture, reflexology.
- Shuttle and private car transportation are provided at no charge.
- Millennial- and Gen Z-focused language and experience.
- Multilingual website, patient forms, live chat, and team members
- Zero-down financing

Once you are clear on what makes you different or sets you apart, you want to be able to articulate it. This is not the usual "we care" or "we offer quality service" messaging. I'm inviting you to be brave enough to look at what truly makes you personally unique and, therefore, your practice. If you don't already know, ask your patients and team about what they love about you.

As you become clear about whom you want to attract into your circle of influence and why you are special, you can begin to explore the remaining fundamentals of influence.

2. Understand Your Team's or Patients' Fears and Desires

Once you've identified your target audience, it's essential to understand them on a deeper level. By discovering their fears and desires, you can tailor your approach and marketing to resonate with them and attract more of your ideal patients. If you are struggling to connect with your ideal audience, gathering information about their decision-making style or habits can also help you resonate with them.

Through effective marketing, advertising, and branding, you can use your patients' exact language to attract more of your ideal patients, while repelling those who aren't a good fit. After you serve your patients well, some of these patients become your greatest allies, supporters, and referral partners. Remember: if you market to everyone, you're marketing to no one.

3. Stand Out and Connect

The aim of any service is to stand out amongst the rest. By identifying what sets you apart and understanding your target audience, you can grab their attention. But to truly connect with them, you need to tailor your messaging to speak to their desires, fears, and aspirations.

Consider identifying groups or communities that you can offer exclusive incentives to, and forge relationships with strategic partners. When it comes to marketing campaigns, vision, and mission statements, don't be afraid to get creative with your offers.

Remember, just because you're in the dentistry business doesn't mean you can't think outside the box.

For instance, one clever campaign for a dentistry practice involved offering a free poker set to patients who had a free consultation, along with a chance to win a trip to Las Vegas or a luxurious casino resort. Other examples of successful campaigns included giving away a Gucci bag or iPad.

I knew of one dentist who put a child-size, Mini Cooper vehicle for kids in his lobby to encourage people to follow them on social media. Each new follower received an entry in the drawing for the small children's car. They were able to leverage this offer for over six months, building a sizable following. Always remember to comply with the legalities in running promotions.

So, remember to create memorable messaging that speaks to your ideal patients, offer exclusive incentives, and don't be afraid to get creative.

4. Build Credibility and Trust

Establishing credibility and trust is crucial for building influence. This high honor can be easily destroyed if not earned, maintained, and packaged properly. Fortunately, there are many ways to establish credibility, such as earning a title or certification, building relationships, publishing, writing, and hosting a successful podcast. Trust can also be built through follow-through, integrity, and servant leadership.

Multiple management studies have shown the most important criterion employees use when it comes to their manager's credibility and trustworthiness, is consistency. To build trust, influential leaders have the courage and conviction to keep their word, communicate transparently, take responsibility for mistakes, listen deeply, and create personal connections (business appropriate). Maintaining confidentiality when receiving feedback and valuing individuals in your vision goes a long way as well. Celebrating your people publicly and coaching them privately helps to maintain trust because you are treating them with dignity and respect.

Building trust can be as simple as acknowledging people in your lobby to let them know when you're running behind or thanking an employee for something you noticed they did well. Influence cannot exist without trust, making it a critical aspect of success. Trust must be built and then preserved to have a lasting impact.

Tips To Build Trust

In order to establish trust, it's crucial to integrate the following tips into your regular interactions, particularly with new connections and in important situations:

- ✓ Always keep your word, be consistent, and maintain confidentiality.
- ✓ Lead by example.
- ✓ Keep communication transparent, avoid gossip, and address concerns directly.
- ✓ Take responsibility for your mistakes instead of throwing blame.
- ✓ Listen actively and exhibit empathy towards others.
- ✓ Provide incentives that have a personal impact.
- ✓ Request and receive feedback often and provide constructive criticism.
- ✓ Encourage others to be a valuable part of your mission and clearly communicate their role.
- ✓ Thank people, celebrate in public, and coach in private.

Incorporate these practices to foster a bond of trust with others and bolster your relationships.

> **The truth is...**
>
> One can have trust
> without influence.
> Yet one cannot have
> influence without trust.

5. Enroll People in your vision and mission–reinforce and reward

As President Dwight D. Eisenhower once said, "Pull the string, and it will follow wherever you wish. Push it, and it will go nowhere at all." As a leader, you must pull your team forward by crafting a clear and concise vision and involving them in its creation and implementation. When people feel a sense of ownership and pride in their work, they are more committed to long-term success.

To enroll your team in your vision, ask for their input and feedback. Encourage questions and seek to understand their perspectives, concerns, and suggestions. Make sure your vision is memorable and easy to repeat. Communicate consistently and reinforce the importance of their role in the practice's success.

It's also vital to steer your vision continually and make adjustments when necessary. As a role model, demonstrate your commitment to the vision and provide unique incentives to encourage and reward your team's dedication. Throughout my career, I've witnessed numerous incentive programs — but only one truly stands out. In this case, the practice owner offered each employee a percentage of ownership in the business through a 20-year plan. The team worked tirelessly to meet their goal of co-ownership and successfully managed the multi-location practice, consistently investing their personal time to improve the business and patient outcomes.

By documenting their progress, the employees were able to track their journey to ownership, further instilling a sense of accountability, integrity, and loyalty. This level of commitment to the team even enabled employees to self-select to leave if they weren't the right fit. The team was known for taking calculated risks and using their best judgment to make decisions, with the trust and support of their employer.

This incentive program truly redefined the standard of employee ownership and involvement in the success of the business. However, ownership isn't just about financial investment. It's about giving your team permission and authority to try new things and supporting them when mistakes are made. Documenting progress and celebrating milestones can help people see their progress and motivate them to keep pushing forward.

Ultimately, enrolling people in your practice requires a two-way commitment. You must care about your team's success and continually provide value to your patients beyond their regular appointments. Consistency and excellence are paramount to achieving success in your practice, no matter how many competitors you face.

Online you will find *Team Engagement Best Practices Checklist.*

6. Take Responsibility

As a leader, it's essential to take responsibility and avoid blaming others for any shortcomings. If your team fails to support your vision, it's your responsibility to identify what's missing and reflect on how to enroll them in your mission. Accountability lies solely with you.

A real-life example drives home the importance of owning responsibility. A woman being interviewed after a robbery blamed the thieves for the loss of her personal belongings, including her computer and valuable jewelry. However, when pressed about preventative measures such as alarm or camera installation, backing up her computer, or hiding her jewelry, her responsibility in the situation became apparent.

Responsibility is key to building influence and achieving success in any career or practice. When you hold yourself accountable rather than expecting everyone else to be responsible, blame games and resistance to change diminish. By assuming complete responsibility for your business and leveraging your influence, you can enroll others in your mission and empower them to take care of business.

An example of responsibility that most dentists miss is managing online reviews. Always respond to patient reviews online, especially negative ones, as it is a crucial step to maintaining trust and credibility while enabling service recovery opportunities. Remember others are watching how you respond to negative reviews, so this is a great opportunity to shine.

Popular review sites include Google My Business, Yelp, Facebook, Yahoo Local, and Nextdoor, with dental-specific sites such as Vitals, 1-800 Dentist, Dentists, Dentistry, Healthgrades, and RateMDs are all consistently growing their audience.

7. Collaborate with Others

Collaborating with others is a powerful way to achieve your goals quickly and efficiently. Team up with individuals who possess the skills and influence you need to speed up your success. Offer your own skills and influence others who want to work together.

Look to your network for potential collaborators, such as associates, vendors, sponsors, investors, bankers, and senior executives. To ensure a successful collaboration, define the parameters of success. This may include financial expectations, timelines, stakeholders, goals, metrics, and specific language.

For example, ABC Bank and All Things Dental are collaborating on a co-branded marketing campaign to gain more exposure to a new market, Lionville, for both companies. On July 7-10 we will participate in the Lionville Family Fun Fair with an event booth with both brands being promoted. Each of us will provide 20-minute educational presentations as part of their family education sessions. Our collective goal is to build an email list of at least 300 new people and schedule at least 20 banking appointments and 20 dental appointments. We will each provide a free copy of our book to anyone who joins our email list or provides their name, address, and phone number on their raffle ticket at our booth. Collaborate for success and see how far you can go.

Navigating Successful Collaborations

Define Success

Be clear about the definition of success. Examples of important components to include in the definition of success are any combination of the following:

- ✓ Financial Expectations
- ✓ Timelines
- ✓ All Who Benefit
- ✓ The "Why" Behind the Collaboration
- ✓ Goal(s)
- ✓ Metrics to Measure
- ✓ Specific Language

Set Clear Expectations

Write out a detailed list of the expectations for each party. Expectations may include any combination of the following, or additional unique items.

Financial:

- Identify the cash, products, and resources each party is investing
- Decide who has the authority to make binding agreements and spend money

Ground Rules:

- Clearly define roles and responsibilities for each party
- Decide how decisions will be made when two parties are at an impasse
- Establish ground rules and/or behavioral standards

Timeframes:

- Specify deadlines and details for deliverables
- Detail projected dates of periodic milestones for the project

Harness the Power of Influence to Achieve Your Dreams

When used strategically, influence can help you achieve your *Wheel of Life* goals faster, build strong relationships, and create collaborative opportunities. Cultivating your influential leadership skills across all areas of your life can lead to a more meaningful, connected, and rewarding life, a legacy, personal growth, and even financial rewards. Don't let the time freedom you dreamed of slip away. Become a trusted, influential leader and make your vision a reality.

With Patients

Dr. Sean expertly guides implant dentistry patients through case acceptance and onboarding, empathetically tuning into their desires, fears, and aspirations for achieving a beautiful new smile in just one day.

"I spent years looking for the right dentist!"
—Natalie Vasquez

"I had looked at many places for many years to find an implant dentist who could help me. When I found 4M and Dr. Sean, they were honest and straightforward, and very informative, which was a big part of my decision to go with Dr. Sean. The staff was welcoming and made me feel comfortable with the treatment. I had two bone grafts, two zygomatic implants, and the All on 4 implant procedure.

The process was easy, and the procedure was painless. The two-day recovery was painless, and they checked on me several times. This procedure changed me completely. I am a whole new person. In fact, having lived this as a patient in a first-class way inspired me to finally pursue my dream of working in a dental practice. I have now been a dental assistant in a pediatric dental practice for almost a year."

With Your People

As an employer, it is crucial to grasp the desires, fears, and aspirations of your potential hires and associate dentists who are eager to join your practice. Gaining this understanding sets the foundation for a successful and fulfilling working relationship.

With Relationships

This influence model applies to relationships as well. For example, when it comes to co-parenting after a divorce, it's important to put your children at the forefront of your thoughts. By considering their desires, fears, hopes, and dreams, you can create a new model for your family that's centered around them. Additionally, you should have open discussions with your ex-spouse about their own goals for healthy, low-stress co-parenting.

Remember, the influence and impact you have on those you serve, support, or collaborate with is equally important as it is for achieving your own goals and lifestyle.

Scan the QR Code below with your smartphone
Or go to https://youtu.be/tXIAhWJPECw
for a message about Influence

Chapter 6
REFLECTION:
The Power of Influence

1. Which one of the **Seven Influence Fundamentals** is my strongest personally? Strongest for my practice?

   7 Influence Fundamentals

   1. Identify Your Ideal Audience and What Sets You Apart
   2. Understand Your Team or Patients' Fears and Desires
   3. Stand Out and Connect
   4. Build Credibility and Trust
   5. Enroll People in Your Vision and Mission–Reinforce and Reward
   6. Take Responsibility
   7. Collaborate With Others

2. Which one of the Seven Influence Fundamentals is my greatest opportunity as a leader and for my practice?

3. As an influential leader, do I create instant credibility and trust with others? What improvements can I make personally and for my practice? Refer back to *The Tips to Build Trust* list.

4. In what ways am I leading by example and taking responsibility for our success without blaming others?

5. Is my practice "leading by example" in the community (community service, fundraising, sustainability, environmental impact)?

6. With whom could I be collaborating in our community for the benefit of our patients' experience?

Chapter 6
ACTION:
The Power of Influence

1. Informally or formally survey members of your leadership team and your staff to learn from their input and feedback how you might improve your influence skills as a leader in terms of your practice.

2. When presented with feedback on how you could improve yourself or the practice, ask for suggestions on what to improve, e.g., ask what you could stop, start, or continue doing to improve.

3. Based on the Influence Fundamental you decided to improve upon (see REFLECTION on the previous page), create your own improvement plan. Determine the one specific action you will take to begin improving. Then commit to weekly and monthly actions to reach your goal 90 days from now.

4. Make a list and prioritize the people and organizations with which you could collaborate over the coming year. Create a plan to communicate with each one to explore opportunities to collaborate.

5. Review your website(s) and your social media messaging to identify strengths and opportunities in terms of influence and brand reputation. View your site from the perspective of a new prospective patient. Does your site adequately convey your vision, mission, values, "why," and what makes you and your practice truly unique?

The following tools are available here:
www.TheresNoStandingStill.com

Stop Start Continue Checklist
Successful Collaboration Checklist
Team Engagement Best Practices Checklist
Patient Engagement Best Practices Checklist

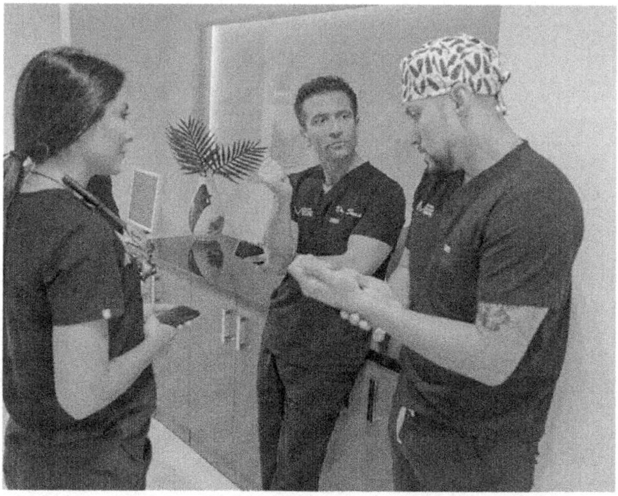

Your People

CHAPTER 7

Retaining Valuable Team Members

"Am I teaching, mentoring, and making time for each of my team members?"
—Dr. Sean Mohtashami

Although dental school teaches the ins and outs of practicing dentistry, it doesn't prepare us for the leadership and management aspects of running a business. Unfortunately, we are on our own to figure this all out. Initially, straight out of dental school, I was a bit like my dad, a bit rough, and did not know how to thank people. But I quickly learned that if I do not show genuine appreciation for my people, they will not stay with me, no matter how much money I pay them.

As a first-generation immigrant from Iran, I've learned firsthand how to work hard and provide for my family. However, when it came to hiring employees, I was surprised by what I saw. Why are some employees not willing to work hard? Why are they not willing to sacrifice for their coworkers and our patients?

I believe that showing our employees genuine appreciation is necessary, regardless of how much we pay them. I put in a hundred percent of my effort every day, striving to achieve excellence, and I don't understand why some people choose to cut corners and work less. It's frustrating for me as an employer to see my team members not living up to their potential and rob us of the value we agreed upon during hiring. Meanwhile, their coworkers are putting in their time and working hard.

Although I have a soft spot and tend to give people multiple chances to improve, I eventually come to the realization that it's time for some team members to move on. It's difficult for me to have patience and compassion for employees who are not willing to work hard, but I know that investing time and effort in the right people can yield great results.

Powerful Lesson: Addressing Non-Performers

As a business owner, you may have the best intentions for your team members, but one mistake could negate everything you say. When an underperforming staff member is left unchecked, it sends the message that you do not care about those who are working hard and dedicated to the work.

This simple yet powerful lesson dawned on me after my superstar team members raised concerns regarding an employee who had been given plenty of chances to improve but showed no change. They said that I was having a negative impact on our working environment, which undermined the message that I care about them.

It is never easy to terminate an employee, but you owe it to your team members to act when necessary. Remember that good employees are hard to find and keep, and their loyalty should be reciprocated with fair pay, respect, and a great workplace. Pay them more than is typical in the industry and reward them for great performance.

Retaining people makes more sense than starting all over again with a new hire merely for a couple of dollars an hour. Take care of your team members, and they will never want to look for another job. This decision has been one of the best I have made in my business.

> Find good employees and take care of them – pay them fairly, treat them with respect, solicit their input, and honor their expertise.

More Than Just Money

Teaching and mentoring have been a significant source of motivation, meaning, and purpose throughout my career. Recently, one of my team members resigned after a decade of working together. Though it was difficult, reflecting on our time together made me realize the value we brought to each other's lives. She shared how she had learned more from me and our team than from any other medical office she had worked in before and expressed gratitude for the experience. When team members like her leave, I am excited for their future endeavors and proud of the skills, talents, and potential they possess.

As a mentor, my top priority is ensuring that my team members learn and grow both professionally and personally. I ask myself if I have contributed to their growth and development, if I have taught, mentored, supported, or spent quality time with them. When team members are committed to excellence, eager to learn, hustling, and humble, we have an opportunity to work towards something truly unique. Working together, we can achieve something outstanding and unforgettable, delivering "Wow" experiences to our patients.

Our efforts extend far beyond merely providing dental services – we are changing the lives of our patients and our team members.

The most rewarding aspect of my journey is knowing that many individuals have learned and grown because of what we have achieved together. Our mission is about more than just filling cavities; it's about changing the lives for our patients and our team.

> Our mission is about more than just filling cavities; it's about changing the lives for our patients and our team.

Employee Engagement

Employee engagement is a crucial factor in the success of any organization. As such, it is vital to know the effective ways of increasing this engagement level among employees without incurring any cost. According to multiple research sources, including a report by the Society for Human Resource Management (SHRM), the following are seven ways to achieve this feat.

Firstly, supply the right tools to your employees. Ensure that they have the necessary equipment and resources to perform their duties efficiently. Secondly, give your employees individual attention. Show them that you recognize their unique efforts and contributions to the company.

Thirdly, provide training and coaching for your employees. Continual learning and development not only benefit the employees but also enhances their productivity and engagement level. Fourthly, listen to your employees. Encourage them to express their opinions and ideas.

Fifthly, get social in a business-appropriate manner. Organize company events, team building activities, or virtual meetings that foster interaction and collaboration. Sixthly, serve others through servant leadership. Support and empower your employees in achieving their goals.

Lastly, recognize proudly and loudly. Celebrate the success of your employees publicly and provide private coaching where necessary. Implementing these no-cost strategies will result in a more engaged and motivated workforce, thus increasing your organization's success.

The seminal study in employee engagement was conducted by Gallup which resulted in the Gallup Q12 survey on employee engagement. You will find plenty of resources online.

Knowing When to "Push" Your People to Achieve Their Best

Not every member of your team may be a star player. Some may be there just for a paycheck, while others are good but not exceptional at their jobs. Some are working towards a future in healthcare or a different career altogether. Regardless, it is important to know how to motivate and engage each team member for their own professional growth, and the benefit of your patients. While understanding their life experiences, education, maturity level, behavioral style, strengths, and personality type can help, it's best to start with the fundamentals.

When you find a team member with a true commitment to learning and development, you can positively impact their life and contribute to your own legacy. For those open to challenges and growth, pushing them outside their comfort zone may lead to excellence. Several tell me they love the challenge and learning, and appreciate the investment made in their development.

Challenging High Performers

Throughout my experience, I have discovered effective ways to challenge high performers and support their personal and professional growth. Here are a few of the best ways to encourage progress in your high performers:

Consistently schedule one-on-one check-ins with your high performers. Make time for them, even if it's only for a few minutes. Every bit counts.

Engage them with thought-provoking questions, such as "What did you learn today?"

Provide direct and constructive feedback to help them improve.

Ask for their input on how to enhance performance, using questions such as "What could we start/stop/continue doing?"

Encourage them to demonstrate what they have learned and showcase their progress.

I'm reminded of my teenage years learning Shotokan Karate, where the journey to black belt begins with white belt "at the top" and black belt "at the bottom" because our instructors "pour into the student" and the student grows.

Loyalty

At the core of our team's success lies the importance of family, a lesson instilled in me by my parents. As professionals, we spend countless hours working alongside our colleagues, forging bonds that become like a second family. Our full-time team members each invest over 2,000 hours per year working together, caring for patients and their families, and ensuring that we all learn and grow along the way.

At the heart of our relationships is trust and loyalty. I strive to ensure that all team members feel supported and valued, sharing the highs and lows of our daily work life. Loyalty goes far beyond arriving on time and completing assignments. True loyalty is demonstrated by not only supporting the business, but also by being there for each other, even through difficult times.

In my years of experience, I have learned that loyalty is represented through certain characteristics and actions. I aim to cultivate these qualities in myself and my team, building a foundation of trust and support that can withstand any challenge.

The Loyalty Self-Assessment Checklist is available at: www.TheresNoStandingStill.com

Retaining Valuable Team Members

I've discovered the key to retaining great staff through trial and error. What helped me the most was hiring coaches to develop my leadership effectiveness and implement best practices for employee retention. The hiring process is crucial for building a successful team, but it's only the beginning. How you treat and onboard new hires sets the tone for lasting success.

Consistent effort in soliciting their input, showing them appreciation, teaching, coaching, and mentoring, creates trust and loyalty. Quick addressing of staff issues is also crucial for maintaining trust, loyalty, and focus on patient satisfaction.

While paying competitive wages is important, it's not the only factor in keeping good people. How we treat our people and keep them engaged and connected is the secret to lasting success.

Check out the *Six Staff Retention Drivers and Retaining Valuable Team Members Inventory* for a list of best practices in engaging and retaining your people.

***The Great Leader Conversation Starter Guide* provides valuable insights for connecting with your team.**

Understanding Dental Associates

Working with Associates has taught me valuable lessons. While they may not necessarily have an entrepreneurial mindset, they all share a goal of becoming exceptional dentists. The key is to motivate and empower them to push beyond their comfort zones.

To maintain my sanity and happiness while building multiple practices, I have realized that each Associate has their own pace and aspirations. My role is to understand their needs, fears, and insecurities, and to support them little by little in their development.

To succeed in growing the practice with multiple offices, it is crucial to continually assess the fit of each Associate. An even better approach, as taught by the Disney Institute, is to thoroughly assess potential Associates during the interviewing and hiring process to ensure the right fit for the speed of growth of your practices.

Chapter 7

REFLECTION:
Retaining Valuable Team Members

Simply ask yourself...

1. Do I pay my people what the job is worth, what they are worth, or the amount that will keep them from ever thinking about leaving to take another job?

2. If I could change any one thing immediately about how we retain our best employees, I would change ______________.

3. Regardless of how much I pay my people, do I show them a genuine appreciation for what they do? Do I show appreciation often enough?

4. Do I solicit input from all of my team members on a regular basis, not just in times of crisis or challenge? (at least as many team members as possible)

5. Am I teaching, mentoring, and making time for each of my team members? If not, what are my excuses?

6. If one of my 10-year team members resigned today, what would they say they learned from me? From our team?

7. Am I demonstrating loyalty to my team members? Which of my relationships would benefit from completing the Loyalty Self-Assessment?

Chapter 7
ACTION:
Retaining Valuable Team Members

1. Ask your entire team to identify their favorite ways to receive appreciation at work.

2. Review the *Great Leader Conversation Starters Guide* and make a list of employees you get to meet one-on-one to have a meaningful conversation and share your appreciation with them.

3. Identify 3 or 4 of your best team members and for each one, make a list of what you can do or say to them to "re-recruit" them by letting them know how valuable they are to your practice, and ask them for input on improvements for patients and for co-workers.

4. Carve out time in your calendar to make time to spend with individual team members. What can you teach them? What do they want to learn? How can you invest in them, so their job is a meaningful career, not "just a job?"

5. Make a short list of the specific behaviors you get to improve related to being loyal to others. Outline action steps you can take, just a few minutes each day, to improve loyalty.

The following tools are available here:
www.TheresNoStandingStill.com

Great Leader Conversation Starters Guide and Checklist

Loyalty Self-Assessment Checklist

Six Staff Retention Drivers and Retaining Valuable Team Members Inventory

Team Engagement Best Practices Checklist

How to Accelerate Your Hiring and The Best Interview Questions Checklist

Dental Associates Interview Template

CHAPTER 8

Mastering the Art of Asking Better Questions

What makes the difference between a millionaire and a billionaire?
"Delegation."
—Sir Richard Branson

Micromanaging stifles the growth of your people and your business. By constantly wanting things done a specific way and taking over tasks, dentists limit their potential as entrepreneurs. This is a great way to create a job for yourself as a dentist, rather than becoming an entrepreneur who happens to be a dentist.

In a recent conversation with another dentist, he said, "I keep getting phone calls about stuff that I just can't believe my staff are calling me for the answers." He then shared that he was thinking, "You can't make that decision?"

I listened patiently and then asked him, "Have you ever sat with them for 15-20 minutes and shown them why you think the way you do or why you make decisions the way you do?" And he replied, "Well, that's a really good question."

For several years straight out of dental school, I found myself giving team members instructions (routine tasks not a new skill), and then answering their questions every step of the way and following up with them before they had a chance to get back to me to let me know they had taken care of the task. Over time, I became frustrated with why I had to keep teaching and re-teaching the same employee, the same thing.

Worse, I was frustrated why my team members struggled to "see the problem the way I see it" or "figure out the solution on their own."

I kept thinking, why aren't these folks learning how to deal with these issues on their own?

Finally, one day, after a conversation with a peer and a business coach, I realized:

> Whenever I keep answering all my team members' questions, I rob them of the opportunity to learn for themselves, how to do something, and more importantly, rob them of learning critical thinking skills and *"how to think"* about the task, problem, or solution.

My breakthrough was realizing the ROI of an investment of a little extra time upfront— asking them better questions, making sure they understood the *why* and the *value* behind what I was asking them to do, and letting them struggle on their own a bit to come up with their own answers. This helps them learn how to think differently and address the task with more ownership, rather than just relying on me to answer every single question along the way.

This is much easier said than done of course, especially when you are rushing between patients, meetings, taking calls, and following up on previous patients, checking email, dealing with supplies inventory, and dealing with employee issues.

Therefore, I figured out a few best ways to help my team members learn, ultimately, so I could delegate more to them with the confidence of knowing they will handle things correctly.

- Take note of tasks or issues that keep coming up repeatedly–Pick one to address with the team each week
- Host a 5- or 10-minute huddle with the relevant team members, asking them for suggestions or recommendations
- Ask questions of them…avoid the temptation to tell them the solution even when you are "crazy busy"
- Invite them to come up with the solution for this issue that keeps coming up, and present their recommendations to you
- Let them do a "trial" of their solution
- Upon success with the "trial," ask them to document the process and add it to your communication and/or training procedures

The Power of Discovery Questions

Let's look at a typical issue that arises over and over, until the root cause is identified, and a solution is put in place and adhered to consistently from then on.

> **Example:** Team members frequently complain they can't find supplies in the inventory closet.

Instead of doing what seems to be *the easy thing to do,* and just tell them exactly what to do to fix the problem, ask them to come up with the root cause of the issue, and recommend a solution. Teach some of the following discovery questions to your leaders and your staff and let them use the questions to work through a specific issue or challenge they are having.

Useful Discovery Questions to Ask Your Team Members

- ✓ What are all the possible reasons XYZ is currently happening?
- ✓ Who are all the people/roles involved in making this happen?
- ✓ When does the problem happen most often?
- ✓ Where is the problem happening most often?
- ✓ What is the real problem? Are we addressing the "correct" problem?
- ✓ Are we asking the right question(s)?

There are more discovery questions available in the *Discovery Questions to Ask Your Team Members Checklist* online.

Another great technique is to help the person see the issue from another perspective than their own. Ask them, "So if you were another person involved in this instead of you, what would that person say or recommend?"

Finally, ask the individual or group of team members, "If you were the owner of this practice, what would you do?" Or asked a different way, "What would you do if you were me?"

Many Benefits from Discovery Questions

Asking these questions provides a bunch of benefits, both short-term and long-term. Here are benefits we have experienced whenever we engage our team members (challenge them and/or delegate to them) to find the solutions. Employees feel trusted and valued for their opinion and contribution. They feel respected because you are asking for their input. They feel empowered because they are now part of the solution.

These problems are resolved "once-and-for-all" reducing dysfunction, improving outcomes, increasing productivity, and reducing stress. Over time, employees stop coming to you with their questions, and instead, rely on one another to find the answers or create solutions. You may witness emerging leaders from within your team who step up as leaders during this entire process. Time savings for everyone, especially you, are created, and last if the team continues to practice the new solution.

Questions For Checking in With Your Team Members

Once you and your team have agreed upon and implemented the new procedure, new process, or whatever type of solution it is, check-in with your team member(s) using any of these check-in questions. Your goal is to ensure they understand and are committed to the solution.

- ✓ Do you understand why we are doing ________?
- ✓ Are you perfectly clear about ___________?
- ✓ Are you comfortable with ____________?
- ✓ Do you agree with our solution?
- ✓ Do you think this new approach will solve the problem? Short- and Long-term?
- ✓ Can you accomplish this as we have discussed it?

Facilitate Breakthroughs

Another proactive approach to grow your people professionally and personally, which in turn often enables you to delegate more tasks and responsibilities to your team members, is to facilitate "breakthroughs" with your team members or the team.

Thomas Leonard, founder of CoachU, developed the following questions and follow-up questions to facilitate a breakthrough. All along this journey to a breakthrough, are great chances for your team members to grow and develop their critical thinking skills.

7 Questions to Facilitate a Breakthrough with Others

1. What's the breakthrough you'd like to have with this (problem, issue, concern, opportunity)?

2. What needs to happen for this breakthrough to occur?

3. If you knew the answer, what would it be? (Follow up Question, please tell me the first thing that comes to mind.)

4. What's in the way of you taking the next step or making a decision on this?

5. What do you gain by staying stuck or not taking action?

6. If you were advising a coworker about this situation, what would you say?

7. What's the next action you could take based on our discussion?

Follow Up Questions to Ask

1. Tell me more about that (a prompt more than a question)
2. What did you just discover?
3. What are you presenting now?
4. How would that make a difference?
5. What would achieving this breakthrough mean to you?

Your Big Opportunity

If you want to break free from being a *Dentist with a job* and become an entrepreneur or business owner who just happens to be a Dentist, then you must work smarter not harder. Instead of micromanaging everything and everyone, begin to teach your people how to think so they can eventually make informed decisions on their own. Or don't and you will be the *lid on the container* that is holding back your people and your business.

Begin to teach your staff some of the Discovery Questions and how to find the root cause of an issue, challenge, or opportunity. Give them an issue to work through and check in with them periodically. Let them struggle through it.

Use the Check-in Questions to observe and learn how they are doing along the way. When you can help a team member or a small group of team members work toward their own breakthrough, use the 7 Questions to facilitate a breakthrough.

You can download the entire *Discovery and Breakthrough Questions Guide* online on our resource page listed at the end of each chapter.

Chapter 8

REFLECTION: Mastering the Art of *Asking Better Questions*

Simply ask yourself…

1. When talking with my staff, how much time do I spend telling and instructing, versus asking questions?

2. What are some of the issues or challenges that keep coming up because we simply have not invested the time to answer several of the Discovery Questions, or do the Root Cause Analysis work?

3. How often do I keep intending to check-in with my people but then miss the opportunity? (Another reason they are not learning how to think differently)

4. Which individual or team do I get to have a check-in conversation with this week?

5. Which individual or team do I get to have a *breakthrough* conversation with this week?

6. Out of my formal and informal leaders throughout my practice, who are the people (1-3) I get to invest some time with to discuss the use of Discovery Questions and to identify a lingering issue or challenge that we could have a small team begin to work on from Discovery to Check-ins, to Root Cause, to Check-ins, to Breakthrough/ Implementation of their recommended solution(s)?

Chapter 8
ACTION:
Mastering the Art of *Asking Better Questions*

1. Give yourself the gift of personal time to explore your own Discovery Questions:

    - What's working well for me right now?
    - What am I most excited about in my life right now?
    - Where do I need clarity in my life?
    - What do I get to say "No" to this month? This quarter?
    - What distracts me the most in life right now? How do I minimize these?
    - Who can help me accomplish what I want to accomplish this year?
    - What specific acts of self-care do I get to start prioritizing and practicing?

2. Make a prioritized list of the lingering issues or challenges you would like to see your leaders and staff take on using the Discovery Questions in this chapter. Discuss this list of priorities with your Office/Practice Manager and schedule the first short meeting with two or three team members who you will invite to take on a single issue, challenge, or opportunity to explore the root cause and suggested resolution or recommendations for next steps to take.

3. Identify a specific aspect of your life where you would like to achieve your own breakthrough. Explore these breakthrough questions and then meet with your own coach, mentor, or advisor to strategize and create a personal action plan.

7 Questions to Facilitate a Breakthrough for Yourself

1. What's the breakthrough you'd like to have with this (problem, issue, concern, opportunity)?

2. What needs to happen for this breakthrough to occur?

3. If you knew the answer, what would it be?

4. What's in the way of you taking the next step or deciding on this?

5. What do you gain by staying stuck or not taking action?

6. If you were advising a coworker about this situation, what would you say?

7. What's the next action you could take based on our discussion?

The following tools are available here:
www.TheresNoStandingStill.com

Discovery and Breakthrough Questions Guide

CHAPTER 9

Feedback Fuels Team Success

"People don't argue with their own data."
—Bob Pike

Gain valuable feedback and drive your practice's success by utilizing two proven exercises with your team members. These exercises encourage feedback, insights, and recommendations from your team members, leading to better solutions, policies, and practices. By involving your team in these discussions, you'll foster a more collaborative work environment and gain more buy-in for your organization's success.

When introducing new processes or policies, involving your team leads to greater buy-in and investment in their success. Your team will feel like co-creators when they work alongside you and see their input put into action.

These feedback exercises are essential for improving your practice, and their value extends beyond the data they provide. As a leader, soliciting input from your team is essential in creating a successful practice.

Team Member Feedback Exercise #1

Stop, Start, Continue & Mad, Glad, Sad

Based on 25 years of change management consulting, the single most powerful exercise you can do with your team is *Stop, Start, Continue & Mad, Glad, Sad*. You learn a great deal from your team members' feedback in this exercise. Some 50-60% of the data you will "already know," and the rest will be "new" or "expressed in a unique way." You will also possibly realize the scale or severity of an issue impacting your team that otherwise you may have thought was smaller, less common, or less important, e.g., when 80% of your team members say, "The biggest problem we have is XYZ and it has been a problem for years," it is hard to ignore or deny this data, their experience, or perspective.

The critically important issue is for you to respond to the team within seven to ten days of receiving their feedback. The entire process for collecting the feedback is covered in a chapter of the book, *Success from the Inside Out,* by Steven Rowell, entitled "*Stop, Start, Continue & Mad, Glad, Sad.*"

Two of the more powerful and effective tools to use in soliciting feedback from team members are Stop, *Start, Continue & Mad, Glad, Sad.*

Some of the most common situations in which to use these tools are:

- Team Building with staff or management teams
- Soliciting feedback from front-line staff
- Facilitating constructive coaching conversations with an individual
- Discussions with almost anyone when your need is to discover the "real issues" of a situation or a relationship

Stop, Start, Continue & Mad, Glad, Sad can be completed in private by groups of individuals, in dialogue with an individual, or as an interactive team exercise for an entire team simultaneously (using paper or flipcharts for data capture).

A traditional example of using Stop, Start, Continue with a group of employees, is to pass one copy of the Stop, Start, Continue form to each participant. Then ask everyone to quietly, with no discussion, read through the handout and then ask them to write down their responses to the following questions privately using the Stop, Start, Continue handout. You could then facilitate a group discussion, asking individual participants to share whatever they are comfortable sharing in discussion with the entire group.

This *Stop, Start, Continue* form can be used with individuals in private one-on-one conversations as well as being a tool to guide your discussion. You could send the form to the person in advance of your meeting as well if this makes your face-to-face time more meaningful and efficient.

Another method of using this *Stop, Start, Continue* process is to bring a group of ten to twelve employees or managers together (traditionally this is not used with managers and staff in the same group—at least in the beginning of your use of this process). Using flip charts around the room, one labeled STOP, one labeled START and one labeled CONTINUE; you simply ask everyone to either approach the flip chart pages and write their ideas down under each category or use post it notes first—with one idea written per post-it, and then ask the participants to place their Post-its ® on the flip chart pages under each category.

There are advantages and disadvantages to each of these data collection methods for Stop, Start, Continue (or Mad, Glad, and Sad).

CURRENT CONCERNS:

What am I MAD about?

What am I SAD about?

What am I GLAD about?

What are my priorities to address?

PERSONAL COMMITMENTS:

What Should I STOP doing?

What Should I START doing?

What Should I CONTINUE doing?

What are the BENEFITS to me?

Team Member Feedback Exercise #2

Co-Creating Behavior Standards

Behavior Standards have become a best practice in industries such as hospitals, senior living, and some manufacturing sectors. They are also referred to as *Standards of Performance*, *Performance Standards*, or *Standards in Practice*. These standards are proudly posted and displayed in public areas for all guests, families and patients to see at any time.

The important opportunity is to invite your team members to contribute their suggestions for the *Behavior Standards* by which they want to operate as a team. This *Behavior Standards* process, and tool, has been implemented successfully in at least 3000+ companies nationwide. The entire process for collecting the feedback is covered in a chapter of the book, *Success from the Inside Out,* by Steven Rowell, entitled "*Tips for Designing and Implementing Behavior Standards.*" This book is available on the resource page online for your use.

Between Steven Rowell's consulting firm and one other firm, 3300+ of the 6600 hospitals in the US have behavior standards proudly displayed in their lobbies and patient hallways hospital wide.

The payoff for doing this process with your team is a positive impact on the patient experience, enhancement to your company culture, and the self-policing (by patients and staff) of standards that organically comes from the public display of standards.

More payoffs include:

Employee Engagement and Retention

- Increased engagement by asking for their input
- Reduction in negative behaviors between staff

- Team members begin to get more peer-to-peer feedback and encouragement to improve their behaviors/performance
- Less infighting, complaining, snitching, gossiping or triangulation among teams

Peer-to-Peer Accountability

- More consistent adherence to standards because of *self-*policing by staff
- More one-on-one feedback between coworkers with greater *ownership*
- More consistent focus on delivering excellent patient experiences

Patient Experience

- Empowerment of patients who become more likely to speak directly with staff members

Team and Leader Development

- Practice Manager gets a break, to varying degrees, from no longer being a traffic cop, or babysitter, and instead spending more time leading and coaching.
- Supervisors, Leads, emerging leaders, and informal group leaders may *grab the brass ring* of leadership by stepping up and being even more of a role model of standards.
- All leaders gain more courage to hold peers and subordinates more accountable to consistent practice of the behavior standards.

By implementing behavior standards, non-productive time due to conflicts, misunderstandings, and passive aggressive behavior can significantly decrease. Reinforcing one standard per week in morning huddles and team meetings and posting it in visible areas like team member break rooms, highlights the importance of performance improvement and a lasting cultural change in your practice. Remember, investing an extra five to ten minutes on standards can reap invaluable rewards and earn you gratitude from your Practice Manager and Associates for your courage, conviction, discipline, and follow-through. When creating Behavior and Performance Standards, clearly defining language is critical. Training on the specifics of each standard can be done in new hire orientation, new hire onboarding, subsequent training, and annual meetings.

Sample Behavior Standards

Respect**

- *Patients First* is our Focus
- Always respect and honor our employees and dentists
- Model mutual respect by caregivers and leaders

***For example*, you would have a team identify specific behaviors that demonstrate respect as part of this standard—and do this for the other standards too, e.g., Answering, "How do I specifically show respect, and how does the other person know/feel they are being respected?"

Privacy and Confidentiality

- Always maintain confidentiality of patient information
- Respect the privacy needs of our patients
- Always conduct confidential conversations in private

Quality

- Provide exceptional clinical care to every patient we serve (define)
- Fully embrace the *Patient's Right to Know*
- Demonstrate commitment to continuous improvement (be specific)
- Take ownership of patient needs/requests all the way through resolution (teach examples)

Professionalism

- Always serve as a role model of this practice (e.g., *Mother Standard of Care* at Cancer Treatment Centers of America)
- Choose your attitude daily, with patients and guests in mind
- Always look and act the part of a healthcare professional (define)

Safety

- Provide a clean, healthy, and safe environment
- Work smarter, think Safety first
- When you see something, say something
- Wear a mask properly and ensure others do too, at all times

Communication

- Fully explain care procedures to our patients in advance
- Listen to and share information in a timely manner between co-workers
- Language matters in every interaction and every form of communication
- Never respond "I don't know," instead, "That's a great question, let me find out for you...one moment please."

Teamwork

- Provide exceptional timely responsiveness between team members (define)
- No Triangulation between co-workers—go directly to the team member with whom you have a concern, and speak privately with them first
- Assume positive intent (or Assume the Best) of co-workers and patients' communication and interaction

Accountability

- Everyone takes pride in the work we do and the services we provide

- Each of us holds ourselves accountable in providing exceptional care to our patients (be specific about how to hold ourselves accountable)
- Each team member is accountable for their own choices (define)

Cultural Sensitivity

- We honor the multicultural diversity of our staff and the community we serve
- We will speak English in all public areas, especially when interacting with patients, unless our patients or their family members require support in their native language

Service

- Consistently seek out guest and patient contact (core standard to Disney Service Excellence)
- Strive to proactively anticipate the needs of patients and visitors
- Assist all people with directions and wayfinding at any time
- Continually raise the standard of excellence in our pre-visit and post-visit communication with patients

Case Studies: Successful Use of Behavior Standards

Examples of best practices for keeping standards alive and practiced consistently:

Warminster Hospital: In the main lobby stands a podium underneath a large, framed display of their behavior standards. On the podium is a hardcover reception-type journal. Every new hire orientation class includes bringing all new hires to this podium, with the CEO expressing the value of these standards, and then each new hire signs their name as their personal commitment to the standards.

Tenet Hospitals have screensaver messages pop up on every hospital computer, whenever a computer goes into idle mode—Each week one standard is reinforced every day on these screensavers, in their daily five-minute huddles and team meetings.

Five-Minute Huddles with team members include one minute discussing the importance of living standards and speaking to one specific behavior of a Standard as reinforcement. Periodically team members are asked to share a recent example of them living the standard or celebrate a co-worker's example.

The Madlyn and Leonard Abramson Center for Jewish Life new hire orientation facilitators perform a skit demonstrating all standards so new hires experience the importance of living these standards, on their first day of employment.

Pennsylvania Dental Practice (three locations) posts a placard on their reception desk that reads, "Today we are especially focused on explaining procedures in advance for every patient. We are committed to providing excellent service and care to all members of our patient Family." Each week the placard is changed to a different standard. They simply printed each standard statement on stationery and swapped the placard each week.

Boston Dental Practice hosts a Chat with Charles (the Dentist owner) once a week at the beginning of the shift; two team members sit with Charles and he discusses behavior standards, asks for input or suggestions for improvements, and celebrates the two team members' practice of standards.

To see the entire process, script, and best practices to implement Behavior Standards, simply download the *Success from the Inside Out Personal Action Guide* from the online resource page—the link is at the end of every chapter.

Chapter 9
REFLECTION:
Feedback Fuels Team Success

Ask yourself…

1. What information do I think I will hear when conducting our first *Stop, Start, Continue Feedback* sessions?

2. If I could change any one thing immediately about how I lead my teams, I would…

3. Which behavior standards would be most helpful for us to improve the patient experience, and our team's communication and collaboration?

    - Patient Experience:
    - Team Communication and Collaboration

4. Which team members would be great champions of the creation of Behavior Standards for our practice? Who would be the best members of this Behavior Standards project team? When would the best time be to kick off this project team?

Chapter 9
ACTION:
Feedback Fuels Team Success

1. Invest some private time to write down the topics or specific items you think your team members will bring up during the Stop, Start, Continue exercise. What topic will you be surprised to hear them bring up (e.g., Stop or Start)?

2. Write down the steps you need to take to introduce, schedule, and conduct these Stop, Start, Continue Sessions.

3. Identify with whom you will discuss the opportunity to have a task force work to suggest the behavior standards for the practice. When will you meet with them? Who will you choose to lead this Behavior Standards Task Force?

4. Feeling especially courageous? Make a list of individuals you would like to receive Stop, Start, Continue feedback from regarding you and your leadership effectiveness (and/or other aspects of your impact). What date will you bring them together to collect their feedback?

The following tools are available here:
www.TheresNoStandingStill.com

Stop Start Continue Checklist

Co-creating Behavior Standards Checklist

Success from the Inside Out Personal Action Guide

CHAPTER 10

Great Leader Conversation Starters to Engage Your Team Members

"To become more effective and fulfilled at work, people need a keen understanding of their impact on others...and direct feedback is the most efficient way for them to gather this information and learn from it."
–Ed Batista
The Art of Self-Coaching

As our practice grew from one office, then two, then three, I spent a greater amount of time each day leading, coaching, and supporting my team members. Growth also brought with it the need for more team leaders, an HR manager, and a General Manager. Along the way we all learned the critical importance of communication at all levels, and we have the scars to prove it. It wasn't always pretty, yet we stuck together and made it through, growing ourselves, every step of the way.

I learned the same level of care, concern, and intention I put into every patient interaction is required of me, even more so, with every team member. Ultimately it is my responsibility to ensure my leadership team members have the tools and training they need to be effective as well.

For 20 years now, we have known that success with employee retention starts with the supervisor or manager, not the team member, according to Gallup's ground-breaking research, published in *First Break All the Rules (1999).* One powerful *truth* that came out of their research, "Eighty-one percent of those surveyed quit their last job because of their immediate supervisor, not the company." If you have a growing turnover issue in one area of your organization, look first at your supervisors and leaders, then your team members.

> If you have a growing turnover issue in one area of your organization, look first at your supervisors and leaders, then your team members.

Unfortunately, still today, the Society for Human Resource Management found that 93% of managers surveyed needed training on how to coach their direct report employees.

Therefore, a great place to start is making time for one-on-one conversations and using a guide with great questions to ask your team members.

The past decade of employee experience research and best practices have produced the following core factors for successful employee engagement, and increased retention and productivity. These factors are the areas of focus for your professional development efforts with your team, especially as it relates to keeping your best people, providing consistent service excellence, and building a team that operates on its own with little supervision from you.

Successful Engagement

The Core Factors of Successful Employee Engagement are:

- ✓ Trust, Rapport, and Feedback
- ✓ Belonging, Purpose, Meaning
- ✓ Happiness, Fulfillment, and Worth
- ✓ Progress and Learning
- ✓ Achievement, Energy, and Collaboration
- ✓ Career Development
- ✓ Continuous Improvement

This chapter offers a convenient collection of field-tested questions organized into six distinct Question Categories, all carefully designed to address the seven Core Factors of Successful Employee Engagement. Before meeting with your team members, take a moment to review each category and select one or two tailored questions to spark conversation. The next few pages feature a variety of proven questions for each category that you can easily incorporate into your discussions.

Choose questions which may help you achieve any of these outcomes, tailored to the team member with whom you are meeting. Outcomes such as:

- ✓ get to know the person
- ✓ learn more about what drives or motivates this team member
- ✓ discover what suggestions for improvement they may offer
- ✓ listen to them so they feel heard, seen and valued
- ✓ surface a specific topic/concern which otherwise may not have been discussed

- ✓ observe the attitude, mood, or mindset of your team member
- ✓ check-in on the level of ownership/responsibility they take for their work

In preparation for this private conversation, you may find it valuable to review this team member's most recent annual performance review or notes from recent performance coaching sessions to inform which categories of questions you use in your private conversation.

Categories for Great Leader Conversation Starters

- Fostering Communication & Feedback
- Discovering People's Key Drivers
- Increasing Trust With Each Other
- Encouraging Participation & Engagement
- Career Development
- Improvement: Our Company & Our Team

Great Leader Conversation Starter BEST PRACTICES

Near the end of every one-on-one meeting, ask,

- "What are two or three specific actions you can take to move forward on what we discussed today, and by when?"

- The leader's role in a one-on-one conversation is to draw out the team member's issues, concerns, and opportunities, by asking questions and then actively listening.

- Don't rush them, schedule at least ten to fifteen minutes for the one-on-one conversation and keep the appointment unless it is ***imperative*** to reschedule. Rescheduling often erodes trust and negatively impacts engagement.

- Share a time you made a mistake or learned a lesson from failing, or simply model the type of response you are looking for from your team member by sharing your own experience, e.g., "I remember a lesson I learned from my first job which was XYZ, and that has helped me in _____ way ever since. What is a lesson you learned from your last four months with us?"

Remember Peter Drucker's sound advice, "Unless commitment is made, there are only promises and hopes, but no plans."

This chapter includes only a few **sample questions** for each category. You can download the entire *Great Leader Conversation Starters*™ *Session Guide and Checklist* online on our resource page listed at the end of each chapter.

FOSTERING COMMUNICATION & FEEDBACK

- What form of communication works best for you? (Visual, Auditory, Tactile)
- Do you prefer email, text, phone call, voicemail, in-person face-to-face?
- Do you feel you are getting enough feedback? How often do you want to receive feedback?

DISCOVERING PEOPLE'S KEY DRIVERS

- What would you most like to be remembered for when you retire/no longer work here?
- What is your best way to start your day and end your day?
- What drives you? What motivates you to come to work each day?

INCREASING TRUST WITH EACH OTHER

- What is the most important thing you have learned in the last year?
- What drains your energy at work? What energizes you at work?
- What's one thing we could change about work for you that would improve your personal life?

ENCOURAGING PARTICIPATION & ENGAGEMENT

- Do you get to do something at work every day that you love? If so, what is it? If not, what can you do about that?
- What's your go-to productivity trick?
- What's one thing we could do differently here to make your work more efficient? …rewarding? …meaningful? … productive?

CAREER DEVELOPMENT

- What work are you doing here you feel is most in line with your long-term goals?
- What do you want to be doing here in 3 years? …5 years? …10 years? How can we help you achieve those goals?
- Do you feel challenged at work? Are you learning new things?

IMPROVEMENT: Our Company

- What's one thing we've "got to do" in the next six months to improve our product/service?
- If you were me, or the CEO, what's the first thing you would change?
- What's the number one challenge at our company right now? Why? What do you suggest we do to address this?

IMPROVEMENT: Our Team

- How could we improve our team meetings?
- Do you feel overworked, under-worked, or just right?
- Do you feel you are on the same page as your team? If not, what needs to improve?

Additional Questions for Great Leader Conversations

FUN "GETTING TO KNOW YOU" QUESTIONS

- Which person, living or dead, would you like to have as your mentor? Why?
- If you could be rid of one of your fears, which would it be?
- What person do you think has had the greatest influence on your life so far?

1-on-1 QUESTIONS TO ASK A MANAGER OR SUPERVISOR

- Do you spend too much time in meetings? If yes, which meetings do you think you should stop attending? Is there someone on your team who could/should attend in your place?
- Divided by percentages, how much of your day, on average, is spent in meetings: managing your team, completing your own work alone, putting out fires/doing work that could be done by others in your department/team, coaching team members? (e.g., 40% meetings; 10% managing team; 20% completing own work; 25% putting out fires/doing work of others; 5% coaching)
- If money were no obstacle, what investment would help you be even more effective as a leader of your team? ("If money were no obstacle," enables them to think bigger and not limit themselves.)

MANAGER ENGAGEMENT & SATISFACTION

- Do I provide enough support and timely follow-up for you?
- What do I need to stop doing or start doing to better support you?
- What feedback do I need to hear that you think no one has had the courage to tell me until now?

MANAGER AS COACH

- Are you able to meet one-on-one with each team member often enough? Why or why not?
- Who are your best performers? Are we providing enough opportunities for them to learn new things, grow their responsibility, or become ready for a promotion?
- Who is struggling or is at risk due to their performance, right now? What action plan is in place?

MANAGER'S TEAM FOCUS

- What are three of your team's biggest successes in the past 30 days? 90 days?
- What is the definition of success for your team—operationally and financially? ...product/service-wise? ... within the team? ...with other teams/departments?
- What are you most proud of about your team right now?

Chapter 10
REFLECTION:
Great Leader Conversation Starters

1. What are all the benefits of investing more time in getting to know my team members? For me? For them?

2. Are my practice manager and team leaders creating and investing time in building relationships with their team members?

3. Thinking of each leader on my team, which of these core factors for successful employee engagement and retention are my greatest opportunities for improvement so, I can support and lead them better? (It will likely be different for each person)

    - Trust, Rapport, and Feedback
    - Belonging, Purpose, Meaning
    - Happiness, Fulfillment, and Worth
    - Progress and Learning
    - Achievement, Energy, and Collaboration
    - Career Development
    - Continuous Improvement

Chapter 10
ACTION:
Great Leader Conversation Starters

1. Make a list of individuals with whom you get to have 10- to 15-minute conversations using these conversation starters. Jot down your intention for having this conversation, and the goal you are hoping to achieve. Then, using the *Great Leader Conversation Starters™ Session Guide*, make a note of the starter question you will use to initiate the conversation, for each person.

2. Meet with your practice manager to discuss how they can use these conversation starters with team leaders and team members alike.

3. Outline a list of "starter" questions you will use when you meet one-on-one with your practice manager, and with each of your associate dentists.

You may find the questions under the categories Progress and Learning; Career Development; and, Continuous Improvement, especially useful.

There is also a resource available for enabling your team members to have meaningful conversations called ***TeamCHATS™***

The following tools are available here:
www.TheresNoStandingStill.com

Great Leader Conversation Starters™
Session Guide and Checklist
Employee Engagement and Retention Checklist (Core Factors)
TeamCHATS™ Success Guide and Checklist

Your Patients

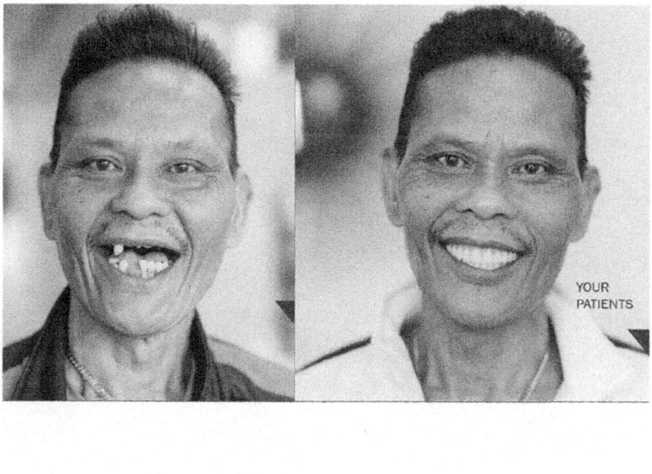

CHAPTER 11

Did You Hear Me? Empathic Listening

"Nobody cares how much you know
until they know how much you care."
—President Theodore Roosevelt

Dentistry is an intriguing blend of art, science, and human interaction. Though dental school may have neglected it, the human component plays a crucial role in the success of a dental practice. Communication is particularly vital, as it is a dynamic part of human interaction that begins with listening. By listening attentively, we open the door to understanding and trust.

As a fellow practitioner, I've discovered that communication breakdowns among team members are a frequent source of tension. Patient satisfaction hinges on our ability to communicate effectively. Becoming self-aware and recognizing our communication limitations involves being present, avoiding interruptions, and genuinely engaging with others to understand their views.

Our hyper-connected lives, complete with smartphones and the internet, make it easy to grow disconnected from those around us. Putting aside our devices and headphones presents an opportunity to be present in the moment and actively listen with understanding. This methodology can lead to increased productivity, improved outcomes, and a reduction of confrontations. By reclaiming the time, we spend focusing on high-value activities, we can achieve greater success in the field, making active listening a key skill in dentistry.

The Magic Five:

Five Minutes that Change Everything

My patients have told me over the years how much they appreciate my approach when I sit down next to them and ask them to tell me their story, their experience, and their desires for improving their smile. My business coach once asked me, "What do you do, or how do you show up, when sitting with your patients?" My immediate response was,

> "I want my patients to feel seen and heard, and to believe they are safe and in good hands with us."

With the help of feedback from my team members, coaches, and patients, I offer you what has worked for me:

- Taking a moment to set my intention for a great patient interaction, before every patient visit
- Clearing my head of any possible distractions before approaching the patient
- Focusing on being fully present with my patient, especially in the first five minutes
- Sitting on a stool next to their chair
- Making eye contact and smiling to help them relax and feel seen and heard

- Not interrupting them, nor looking at my watch or looking away, and sitting calmly
- Investing the time to listen to their fears, concerns, past dental experiences
- Encouraging them to share their desires, hopes, and dreams for their future smile
- Eliciting their thoughts and feelings about how their life will improve with their new smile

I've learned to have tissues nearby because many of my patients feel safe enough to share their deepest feelings about their smile and how it impacts their life and their self-esteem.

"Dr. Sean let me cry and share my story for the first time!"
—Laura Valdez

"I was at a point in my life when I knew I needed implants. I did my research and Google showed me the 4M Dental Implant Center. On my first visit, all the staff were welcoming, and Dr. Sean allowed me to cry and share my story for the first time! Immediately I said, "I want this office to be the one to change my life." Dr. Sean performed my implant surgery first for my upper teeth in December 2019.

Because of the bond I feel with the staff, and the great work Dr. Sean did, I returned in June 2023 to have my lower teeth replaced. Dr. Athena did an incredible job as well. Now I'm back to eating and enjoying food, having a social life, and loving myself."

Empathic Listening in Practice

The rest of this chapter is from my business coach, Steve Sperry, founder of *Inventive Dental Solutions* in Las Vegas, and co-founder/co-facilitator of *Lotus Leadership Event* for dentists. I will share examples of what has worked well for me as well.

To improve your listening skills and have better conversations, start by self-assessing how you spend your time when you are truly engaged in listening. Reflect on this as you read through the following tips.

One way to enhance your conversations with others is by asking open-ended questions that encourage them to share their thoughts, feelings, needs, and desires. By doing this, you create an easy flow for communication and a chance for patients or callers to feel truly heard and seen.

The best conversationalists don't dominate the discussion, and instead focus on listening and making short, concise contributions. Quality conversation is like a ball that is passed back and forth between participants, with everyone getting a chance to speak. Listening is the most important skill for successful conversation, so work on improving it to build better connections with others.

- How often do you find yourself truly present and actively listening for understanding?
- How often do you find yourself interrupting or dominating the conversation?
- And the most common mistake… How often are you just thinking about what you will say next, rather than truly listening?

The following best practices for empathic listening, from Steve Sperry, have been extremely helpful when training our staff. Remember, "Common sense is not always common practice," so we all have ways we can improve.

Four Best Practices for Empathic Listening in a Conversation

These are powerful, practical, and proven techniques to dramatically increase your influence with other people through listening.

Listen Attentively, Without Interruptions

Effective communication starts by valuing what the other person has to say. Being an attentive listener not only flatters the speaker, but it also leads to open and meaningful conversations. Unfortunately, many of us are too focused on preparing a response or waiting for an opportunity to speak, resulting in poor listening skills. To improve our ability to connect with others, we must prioritize understanding over talking.

Active listening involves verbally acknowledging what the speaker is saying, such as with simple responses like "Oh" or "I see." An effective method for establishing connection and building trust is mirroring words, also known as the "echo effect." Psychologists and Neuro Linguistic Programming (NLP) Master Practitioners teach a method of mirroring now known as the "echo effect" which includes repeating back the words one hears from other people. Using the same words makes people feel more similar, less emotionally distant, and more connected. Several studies have shown mirroring people's words can increase people's perception of likability, safety, rapport, and social cohesion. [The Echo Effect: The Power of Verbal Mimicry to Influence Prosocial Behavior, *Journal of Language and Social Psychology* October 14, 2013]

This approach makes people feel understood, resulting in a stronger emotional connection. By employing these techniques, we can quickly establish ourselves as experts and trusted advisors in any relationship.

Interrupting conversations is a natural tendency, but it can hinder your ability to connect with others. To avoid interrupting, consider the context of the conversation and set your intention to listen for understanding. Take note of situations where you tend to interrupt and make a conscious effort to catch yourself in the act. By mastering the art of listening, you can transform your relationships and improve communication with those around you.

In what situations or relationships do you find yourself interrupting the most frequently? What cues can you now look for, or listen for, to "catch" yourself interrupting?

"Dr. Sean saved my life and gave me my confidence back!"
—Jason Yost

"I was born with horrible genetics for teeth. At 17 my teeth started falling apart, decaying from the inside out. Over the years I had low self-esteem and self-worth because of my teeth. I spent twenty years not smiling, ashamed of my teeth. Some people would call me a meth head, or crackhead, even though I never did drugs. I even lost a promotion opportunity because they said I "didn't look the part." One day I became extremely ill from a mouth infection, and I knew if I did nothing, I would probably die. I had been afraid of dentists my whole life. I did initial consults with several dentists, even the big companies advertising on tv, but they never seemed to care if I came back.

Then I discovered All Bright Dental, and my dental anxiety was gone! Dr. Sean allowed me to tell my story and treated me with dignity and respect. Dr. Sean absolutely knows he can change people's lives. The procedure was painless, and the short recovery was too. My new teeth have given me the confidence I had as a kid, and now whenever an opportunity comes in front of me, I know I can go get it! Dr. Sean's life work not only helps people with their oral health, but also their emotional and mental health, which is priceless!"

Pause Before Replying

A short pause of two or three seconds before replying is extremely powerful and engaging. When you pause, you accomplish three goals simultaneously. First, you avoid running the risk of interrupting if the other person is just catching his or her breath before continuing. Second, you show the other person you are giving careful consideration to his or her words by not jumping in with your own comments at the earliest opportunity. The third benefit of pausing is you will more fully hear the other person. His or her words will soak into a deeper level of your mind, and you will understand what he or she is saying with greater clarity. The act of pausing also helps you regulate your enthusiasm or excitement during the conversation. By pausing, you mark yourself as a savvy adept conversationalist.

Ask Questions for Clarification

Never assume you understand what the other person is saying or trying to say. Instead, ask, "***Let me see if I understand you correctly. Can you explain that again?***" This is one of the most powerful questions to use in controlling a conversation. It is almost impossible not to answer. When you ask, "*Can you explain that again?*" The other person cannot stop himself or herself from answering more extensively. Then you follow up with other open-ended questions and keep the conversation moving along.

Paraphrase the Speaker's Words in Your Own Words with Feeling & Emotion

In addition to using mirroring (echo effect), here is another excellent way to navigate your conversation. When replying, periodically you can say, "***Let me see if I've got this right. What you're saying is ....***"

By paraphrasing the speaker's words, you demonstrate in no uncertain terms you are genuinely paying attention and making every effort to understand their thoughts or feelings. When you practice effective listening, other people will begin to find you fascinating. They will want to be around you. They will feel relaxed and happy when they are in contact with you.

- Listening builds trust. This is especially true in phone conversations. The more you listen to another person, the more he or she begins to trust you and believe in you and what you are saying.
- Listening builds self-esteem. When you listen empathically to another person, often their self-esteem will naturally increase.
- Listening builds self-discipline in the listener. Because your mind can process words at 800 words per minute, and we only speak at about 125 words per minute, it takes real effort to keep your attention focused on another person's spoken words. If you do not practice self-discipline in conversation, your mind will wander while listening, and you will miss information or potentially misunderstand it.

The more you work at paying close attention to what the other person is saying, the more self-disciplined you will become. In other words, by learning to listen well, you develop your own character, build your reputation, become more likable, build trust, and make deeper connections with others.

You will discover the many advantages of effective listening, including financial rewards, better patient outcomes, and satisfaction, in the chapter, *The Power of Connecting and Converting Patients Over the Phone.*

Be sure to practice using these questions when listening to others.

> *Let me see if I understand you correctly. Can you explain that again?*
>
> *Let me see if I've got this right. What you're saying is...*
>
> Another helpful statement is,
>
> *Please, tell me more about that.*

There is another area of communication where these skills are critically important as well...in the face of conflict.

Resolving Conflict

A mentor of mine always says, "Conflict, stress, and anxiety within relationships is vastly reduced, first by active listening, seeking first to understand others, then to be understood by others." The reframe, which transforms relationships of all kinds, especially amid conflict, is what he calls, "I care enough about you."

I care enough about you to listen. And I care enough about you to tell you—no matter how difficult the conversation may be.

The next time you find yourself in a conflict with someone, or you wish to strengthen the relationship proactively, simply set your intention as,

"I care enough about them to listen, and to tell them."

This especially helps those whose greatest need is harmony and often struggle to address conflict. *Hint*: As much as 72% of all healthcare workers have a behavioral style in which their core need is harmony. The four behavioral styles are defined, and can be assessed using tools like DiSC, MyersBriggs, or Platinum Rule, just to name a few.

Chapter 11
REFLECTION:
Did You Hear Me? Empathic Listening

1. Simply ask yourself…
   "Which rule of effective listening is my greatest opportunity… a) with patients; b) with team members; c) at home; d) with friends?"
   - Listen Attentively, Without Interruptions
   - Pause Before Replying
   - Ask Questions for Clarification
   - Paraphrase the Speaker's Words in Your Own Words with Feeling & Emotion

2. What need is being met for me when I "do most of the talking" rather than "do most of the listening?" e.g.,
   - I'm the expert; patients don't know what they need and what to ask for so
   - I just tell them; I've been this way all my life; nothing is broken so I don't need to fix anything.

3. Therefore, is this a story I tell myself to rationalize this or, am I now open to improve my listening? (If you are already great at effective listening, congratulations)

4. Do my Associate Dentists listen actively and effectively? If not, what conversation will I have with each one, and by when?

5. Does my practice manager listen actively and effectively? If not, what conversation will I have with them, and by when?

6. Are my call center team members listening actively and effectively? Would improvement in this area improve "first impressions" and/or boost enrollment of new patients?

Chapter 11
ACTION:
Did You Hear Me?
Empathic Listening

1. With whom are you going to practice these two questions more frequently, to improve your communication and your relationship?

   "Let me see if I understand you correctly. Can you explain that again?"

   "Let me see if I've got this right. What you're saying is ...."

   "Please tell me more about that."

2. Who is the one person you will focus on consistently in terms of listening to them more effectively?

   When was your first opportunity to meet with this person?

3. Schedule a one-on-one meeting with my practice manager and each of my Associate Dentists to discuss the importance of effective listening between us, their team members, and our patients.

   By when will these meetings be scheduled?

4. Which team members, especially those in leadership roles who interact with patients, have an opportunity to improve in empathic listening?

   Enroll your general manager or practice manager to share this chapter with these team members, privately.

Then encourage the team members and acknowledge their improved listening skills, whenever possible, after experiencing their improvement first-hand.

The following tools are available here:
www.TheresNoStandingStill.com

Listening Better on the Phone Checklist

CHAPTER 12

The Power of Connecting and Converting Patients Over the Phone

"I've learned that people will forget what you said, people will forget what you did, but people will never forget how you made them feel."
—Maya Angelou

At the end of my new patient appointments, oftentimes I am told, "This is the first time a dentist has truly listened to me," or, "Thank you for spending so much time with me and answering my questions." This is the power of doing *The Magic Five*...those first five minutes when the patient is the most important person in the world to me. Common sense? Sure. Yet doing this every time, with intention, with every new patient, is the key. Consistent practice is the key to providing a "Wow experience" for our patients.

Similarly, phone conversations are your golden opportunity to make people feel heard, seen, and respected. This in turn builds instant rapport, leading to trust and credibility in the patient's eyes. This also sets the stage for me when I sit down for that first time with a new patient. Of course, I do this at the beginning of every appointment, not just with new patients.

Most dental practices are completely unaware of the most valuable asset in their practice—their telephone. Even if your team has had training; even if you record calls, audit them, and coach your people. Even if you think your conversions and show rate are good, you could be missing the most profitable link in the chain. Implant calls can convert to trust and advocacy, not just to appointments.

Your phone system is your most variable link to success. Agents or dealers on the phone can help you reach your best or worst months. The good news is your phone performance is measured, tracked, and easily identified for improvement. It is also the easiest and quickest process to turn around.

A single call can be $25,000—$45,000 in direct income. It's not just the direct value but the lifetime indirect value patients represent. Happy patients send, on average, three others ($75,000—$135,000).

Your call center is often your first contact with patients and guests. This first impression experience is critically important to your success. Your brand reputation is either positively reinforced in this first interaction, or a disconnect is created in the caller's mind. These phone conversations are the foundation of building trust, advocacy, and relationships for your practice.

Essential Tools for Connecting and Converting Patient Relationships Over the Phone

Empathic Listening Skills

As practice owners, we can be a source of reassurance and trust for our patients. One of the greatest gifts we can give a person is to truly listen to them. Instead of just thinking about the next question to ask or how to fix something, we can validate how they are feeling. We can listen for understanding with a "compassionate ear."

Use of Magic Words

In normal times, we make allowances for each other when someone says something abrupt or rude. When under stress, it is significantly harder to deal with a coworker, boss, patient, or family member who upsets us. With some simple word substitutions, we can not only reduce tension but also build confidence and trust, e.g., yes and because; thanks; help; invite you to consider; and using their name.

Trust

Trust is built on the foundation of a personal connection. When a phone conversation is the first touchpoint our patients have with our practices, we must learn how to instantly connect without body language or smiles. The good news is anyone can learn the keys to getting a "YES."

Training for Success

When training your team, it must be a continual training experience throughout the year, every year. Spaced repetition is the key to results. Look at any sport, repetitive muscle memory is king. Plan, plan, plan, execute, then review the result to improve. If you are expecting to find that perfectly trained agent, think again. The best you can hope for is someone with the right attitude. The Walt Disney Company has built its entire global empire with this employee recruitment principle—*Hire Happy, Train for Skill.*

Your call center is most often your first contact with guests and patients—their first impression. At Disney's Central Reservations Office and in their theme parks, attached to every company telephone is a laminated card with the answers to the ten most asked questions which come to that telephone. This way, any Cast Member can pick up the phone with confidence and provide Disney Service Excellence.

"How Do I Get to Your Office?"

If a prospective patient called your office number right now and told your team member, they were new in town and needed directions, what would your team member say? No matter which team member answered the phone, would they consistently be able to ask the patient "From which part of town are you coming?" and then give them directions? Or would they say, "Ma'am, our address 110 Anderson Street comes up on your GPS."

Emotional Intelligence

Just as infection control and safety are essential in our practices, so too is emotional intelligence (EQ). This is something you have control over—while you are born with IQ, your EQ is learned. Seeking first to understand the other person, and then to be understood by them demonstrates high EQ. Emotional Intelligence includes awareness (able to identify and name emotions), harnessing emotions (apply emotions to thinking and problem-solving), and managing emotions (when necessary, adjusting your own emotions, or your reaction to others).

The connection between EQ and Customer Service Excellence is common knowledge today. The Forrester Report study shows that "How a customer feels about a product is more important than its effectiveness." Harvard Business School research established that "Customers are generally led by their emotions; in fact, 95% of all purchasing decisions are made subconsciously." We know patients with positive emotions toward their dentist are more likely to become longer-term loyal patients and make more referrals.

According to NexHealth's survey results published in the State of Dental 2023

> **How Elite Practices Grow 20% Every Year:**
>
> Patient education was the single most important factor in keeping patients engaged and returning to their practices.
>
> Other factors impacting patient engagement and retention were shared decision-making; aftercare; early engagement before the first appointment; and discounts or incentives.

Elements of Great Patient Experiences

These are seven of the important elements to providing great patient experiences with high EQ, while building rapport.

Anticipating Patients' Requests

The core guest service standard taught to and expected of every *Walt Disney World* cast member is, "Consistently Seek Out Guest Contact." The ability to anticipate patients' requests builds trust, demonstrates sincere care and concern, and delights patients by frequently exceeding their expectations.

Delivering Clear Explanations

The PressGaney Patient Satisfaction Survey and the government's HCAHPS Patient Satisfaction Survey ask patients whether staff "Explain in ways the patient could understand." Sharing facts and explaining information, procedures, and instructions clearly, slowly, without jargon, and at the proper point in the conversation are all important facets of clarifying expectations.

Informing and Educating Patients

Like treatment conversations (case acceptance), listening carefully and then informing and/or educating patients fully creates safety and deepens trust in the relationship. Patients appreciate knowing more after a call than when they first placed the call.

Providing Emotional Support

During phone conversations, strive to listen actively, avoid distractions, do not interrupt, ask for clarification, summarize what you just heard, and provide genuine encouragement, reassurance, and compassion.

Offering Personal Information

Avoid the temptation to share your own experiences/stories in a way that takes the focus off them and their experience and feelings at the time. Instead, focus more on listening and asking questions. However, sharing appropriate personal anecdotes quickly does build an emotional connection.

Ensuring Authentic Conversation

Using scripts (key words) for calls helps to standardize the intake conversation, the questions asked, and the conversation. Sticking to the script is important yet you do not want to sound robotic or mechanical. Instead strive for a balance of genuine conversation and key words, phrases, or sentences.

Asking Questions

Questions such as "How are you today?" or "How are you feeling today?" evoke responses that enable you to adapt to the emotional needs of the caller. Clarifying questions ensures you are clearly and fully understanding their needs. Questions create multiple opportunities to emotionally connect with callers.

It's easy to blame others for the lack of our success. There are so many moving parts, so eliminating one big piece of the puzzle lets you focus on all the others. My business coach, Steve Sperry, had a client in Thousand Oaks, CA complain his marketing company was horrible. The fact was his office did not answer calls before 9 AM, during lunch, or after 3 PM. Steve made him a side wager and had his office answer calls 24/7 for several months. He had his best month ever 3 months in a row. We do not dictate when consumers are motivated to move forward with a healthy smile, consumers do! In this age of now, we get to respond to now. It's our job to identify restraining factors to providing service excellence and eliminate them.

Unfortunately, far too often dentists overlook, or worse, ignore the importance of building trust, advocacy, and relationships by phone. The best, most profitable practices, with a great reputation, find the best people because they "Hire Happy," and "Train for Skill" to become masters in delivering service excellence. This team contributes directly and significantly to patient satisfaction, patient throughput, patient referrals, and profitability.

It's the tiny, yet profound, things that make the difference. Remember, big doors swing on small hinges.

Chapter 12
REFLECTION:
The Power of Connecting and Converting Patients Over the Phone

Simply ask yourself…

1. What would "taking inbound new patient prospect calls off the front desk" do for our practice? Our team members? And our patients' experience?

2. What needs to happen or change to improve our ability to connect and convert patient relationships into new patients, returning patients, or patients who refer new patients?

3. Do the phones in our office, especially at the front desk/reception, have the answers to the ten most asked questions next to them so anyone can pick up the phone no matter what role they have on our team?

4. Which metric will improve the most when I and our team focus more on service excellence with telephone conversations?
   - New Patient Appointments
   - Case Acceptance
   - Patient Satisfaction
   - Patient Referrals
   - Coworker Stress Reduction

5. What is my own level of emotional intelligence and the EQ of my team members?

Examples of high emotional intelligence in the workplace are:

- People listen to each other in meetings
- Team members feel safe to express themselves openly
- An upset employee finds a compassionate ear
- People are flexible and embrace change more readily
- Team members take responsibility for their comments and actions
- Blaming others is not a common practice amongst team members
- People being able to move on after making a mistake
- Team members being able to say no when they need to (boundaries)

Chapter 12
ACTION:
The Power of Connecting and Converting Patients Over the Phone

1. Download the two checklists below and identify one specific item you will implement in the next 7 days.

2. Who will put the answers to the ten most asked questions on each of your phones, and by when?

3. Schedule time right now to meet with your practice manager or team members responsible for your call center or phones. Review your success metrics and then decide which specific improvement you will implement and which metric you will track accordingly for the next 60 days.

4. Invite your practice manager and your call center/reception team members to review the seven important elements to providing great patient experiences with high emotional intelligence. Ask them to identify the one element they will focus on for the next 30 days. Ask them to identify one element to focus on each month, for the next six months. When auditing your call recordings, listen for examples of improvement in the element your team is focusing on during that month.

The following tools are available here:
www.TheresNoStandingStill.com

Listening Better on the Phone Checklist
Connecting and Converting Patient Relationships Checklist

CHAPTER 13

Case Acceptance: Think Treatment Conversations

"Listen to their fears, get their dental health backstory, and give them dental advice that connects with them personally–meet them where they're at."
—Steve Sperry

Case acceptance is critical to a dentist's success. Over the years I've been told my own case acceptance track record is excellent. One of the nation's best experts in this area is Steve Sperry, who is the premier dental advisor, coach, consultant, and owner of *Inventive Dental Solutions*.

Steve taught me to think of *treatment conversations* instead of *case acceptance*. This paradigm shift is far more than simple wordplay. The art and science of this shift are key to building a thriving practice.

Lessons Learned

Based on Steve's 25 years of teaching treatment conversations, here are some important lessons learned along the way:

Guide and Lead

The more you push, convince, and sell, the less you will achieve. When you use the laws of attraction, advocacy, and pre-suasion you win (*Pre-Suasion: A Revolutionary Way to Influence and Persuade* by Robert Cialdini).

Relational Not Transactional

The initial contact by phone is your chance to be relational instead of transactional. Relational means listening, understanding, and having empathy for the patient. Transactional is just giving a quote or scheduling the patient without building the relationship and understanding the *why* that brought the patient to the conversation.

Three Best Practices

When scheduling there are three best practices to being relational instead of transactional. Here are three tips for successful conversations:

- Nail the greeting with something different like "How can I brighten your smile today?" or "How can I help you smile today?"
- Get three simple "Yeses" by getting the patient's name and number, then repeating it to the caller.
- Acknowledge they made the right choice. "What inspired you to call us? Great, you will love it here because…"

Handoffs

Effective handoffs between team members, from onboarding a new patient to getting to your "Yes" are invaluable, i.e., the personal emotional connection made with your patient and how this is transferred from one team member to the next. Graceful, seamless handoffs between team members include clear consistent communication, positive energy with empathetic listening, and each team member taking ownership and responsibility for the patient relationship and their experience every step of the way.

We are in the **relationship business**, *not* the Dental Industry. Our goal is to attract and keep patients who like us and trust us. We all agree patient relationships are the key to a successful practice, yet how much time and effort do we invest? Most of our patients do not have the knowledge or experience to make an adequately informed decision about their dental care. Many also have anxiety about going to the dentist in the first place. Therefore, most patients say "Yes," to dental treatment when they trust you, they like you, and they believe you. Your team is integral to building and maintaining this trust as well.

Frankly, the web and social media have enabled your patients to tell the world the good, the bad, and the ugly of their experiences. Therefore, this requires a different level of commitment from you and your team. I invite you to look at your online ratings and reviews (albeit anecdotal data at best). Yet take note of the trends in the data about you and your partner dentists, compared to what is being said about your team. You may discover 5-star ratings of you, yet 3-star ratings or worse of your team members, or vice versa. Therein lies the opportunity to grow.

If We're Transactional, Patients will be Transactional in Return

If we act transactionally, patients will be transactional in return. In my experience, patients ask how much things cost because they do not know the right questions to ask. Price is the easiest question to ask. The trap is answering this question without qualification. If a new patient asks to schedule a new patient appointment and we simply schedule it, we are transactional. If the new patient asks how much it costs, and we answer with an estimate, we are transactional. We do not sell milk or bread. We are not a commodity. We are a relationship-based business. Here are some proven best practices to build genuine trusting relationships with patients and family members.

> We are not selling milk or bread.
>
> We are not a commodity.
>
> We are in the relationship business, not the Dental Industry.

Listening Empathically: One Key to Building Strong Relationships

When we listen, we make an impact. When we listen empathically, patients connect with us. If we do not make time to listen, we reflect a non-caring attitude. If your team cannot listen intentionally to understand the patient's needs, you may be starting a transactional relationship in your first phone contact.

Therefore, the key to better treatment conversations is building better relationships.

Keys to Successful Treatment Conversations:

- Take calls OFF the front desk (truly listen without disruption)
- Hire the right team members (*Hire Happy... Train for Skill*)
- Practice high emotional intelligence amongst your entire team
- Use empathic listening skills consistently

- Train team on the use of "Magic Words" from Tim David's book, *The Science and Secrets Behind Seven Words That Motivate, Engage, and Influence*
- Know and avoid the Three Pitfalls to Failure when scheduling a patient
- Ask great discovery questions (see below)
- ABC (Always Be Converting)
- Record calls, listen, evaluate calls--provide timely coaching (sooner the better)

Our focus must be to help patients get what they are looking for. Listen to their fears, get their dental health backstory, and give them dental advice that connects with them personally--meet them where they're at. When our goal is to help patients do their best, most informed decisions we create win-win-win results and relationships.

Great Discovery Questions for Your Team to Ask New Patients:

- Why are you looking for treatment now? Tell me a little bit about your past dental health and how you got to this point?
- What has held you back from getting treatment in the past?
- What will hold you back from getting healthy? Or getting the smile you have always wanted?
- Have you ever had an amazing experience at a dental practice? Please share what made it amazing for you.
- Poor experience? Please share what made it poor for you.
- If we can give you what you want, make dentistry affordable, and fit a budget you are comfortable with, would you be interested in moving forward?

Different dental industry experts say the average dental practice has nearly $1 million or more of possible treatments hiding away in the patient charts. These treatments have been offered to the patients, but they have not moved forward with them. After completing a thorough review of your patient charts, you will have a list with a variety of possible treatments.

The art and science of conducting effective treatment conversations with patients can add 20%-40% growth to your practice. Therefore, improving this aspect of your patient experience pays significant dividends for years to come.

Scan the QR Code Below to hear Dr. Sean's
Personal Message Recap of this Chapter.

Chapter 13
REFLECTION:
Case Acceptance:
Think Treatment Conversations

1. Think about the 3 best practices to be relational, not transactional, in the initial greeting on the phone.

   Nail the Greeting

   - 3 Simple Yeses
   - Acknowledge They Made the Right Choice

   Which one of these needs the most work in my current process?

2. Thinking of handoffs between team members for the benefit of the patient, what does my team do well, and what do they get to improve?

   This is a great topic for a lunch-n-learn discussion for your team members to identify improvements.

3. When was the last time I, or my practice manager, listened to, and evaluated the recordings of our team members' patient phone calls?

   Are we coaching team members within a couple days of the recorded call, so it is still fresh in their mind? (Or, in some cases, listening to the recording with the team member first)

Chapter 13
ACTION:
Case Acceptance:
Think Treatment Conversations

1. Ask your entire team to identify the Treatment Conversation skills or techniques they *currently use consistently.*

   Ask them, "If you could change any one thing about our Treatment Conversation processes, what would you change?" (Yes, you have seen this question several times)

   Then ask them, "What do we need to Stop doing, Start doing, and Continue doing to improve?"

2. Review the list of ***Great Discovery Questions for Your Team to Ask New Patients*** in this chapter.

   Which one or two questions does your team get to implement over the next 30 days?

   Again, ask select team members to give you their input on these questions too.

3. Identify the one specific best practice to increase your case acceptance rate, that you will implement in the next thirty days.

   Make a list of your greatest opportunities for improvement to work on over the next six months to a year.

   Take time to examine your current case acceptance rates and get clear on the financial impact of improving case acceptance by ten or fifteen percent.

Remember to use this question:

"If we can give you what you want, make dentistry affordable, and fit a budget you are comfortable with; would you be interested in moving forward?"

The following tools are available here:
www.TheresNoStandingStill.com

Great Discovery Questions for Your Team to Ask New Patients

CHAPTER 14

Achieving Service Excellence: Fostering a Culture of Quality Outcomes

"It's not what you do that determines your success, it's how you do it."

Patient satisfaction is achieved by navigating and adapting to the ever-changing expectations of our patients. Consistently delivering service excellence and providing a positive patient experience are paramount to your long-term success. However, identifying the key drivers or best practices to deliver *service excellence* can be difficult. Consistently

- **72% of consumers read online reviews before choosing a healthcare provider.**
- **72% also said they preferred providers who received at least four out of five stars in their reviews.**
- **50% of patients read 10 or more online reviews before choosing a provider while 23% read**
- **20 or more online reviews.**
- **65% of patients say that it's important that providers respond publicly to patient reviews.**
- **94% of consumers say that a negative online review has convinced them not to choose a business.**

delivering service excellence that results in patient satisfaction can be daunting, if not overwhelming, elusive and stress inducing. The good news is there are evidence-based outcomes in patient satisfaction and service excellence in healthcare.

It is important to keep in mind the patient's perception of their patient experience and the level of service excellence provided is what matters to them. You see this every day in online reviews. In fact, according to *the 2022 Healthcare Trends Report*, 72% of consumers read online reviews before choosing a healthcare provider.

My goal is to share what is working well for dental practices today to provide an excellent patient experience and deliver service excellence. Dentistry can learn a lot from acute care hospitals in terms of achieving high levels of patient satisfaction.

I've invited Steven Rowell, a 25-year change management consultant to share the evidence-based outcomes and best practices in patient satisfaction, based on his patient experience improvement system which was licensed for use by more than 1100 hospitals nationwide. Some of these best practices will be brand new to you. Others are *old hat* for your practice. Still others may inspire you and/or remind you of what works. No matter what, I hope you find at least two or three proven tactics, practices, strategies, or methods to significantly improve your patient experience and increase patient satisfaction.

Like when you read a book, or see a movie for the second time, you pick up things you missed the first time or see things from a new perspective. I invite you to read this chapter with an open mind, open to possibilities and new ways of "wowing" your patients.

Evidence-Based Drivers of Patient Satisfaction

Let's first look at the most recent data collected through a variety of surveys in healthcare, including dentistry.

- Average wait time for a Dental patient appointment is 7.5 minutes (Statistia)
- As much as 68%-80% of patients would be less frustrated if they knew how long the wait would be (multiple surveys)
- As much as 41% of patients are willing to see another doctor in the practice to reduce wait time (multiple surveys)

The top five drivers for patient satisfaction resulting in patients writing five-star reviews are quality of customer service (demeanor, attentiveness, helpfulness of staff and practitioners), communication (pre- and post-appointment; reminders; follow-up), and provider's bedside/chairside manner. (PressGaney Feb 7, 2022). Even though this is specifically for hospital patients, it is relevant to dentistry.

According to NexHealth, the top *dental patient* complaint in 2022 was "too difficult to reschedule appointments when necessary."

The other top *dental patient* complaints in 2022 were about the high cost of dental services; too much paperwork; lack of appointment reminders; too much time in the waiting room; and outdated dental office or equipment.

Based on research, evidence-based outcomes, and daily practice, the following are widely accepted in healthcare as the factors with highest correlation to high patient satisfaction (e.g., *PressGaney, Huron, Deloitte, McKinsey, Reconnect*):

Service:

- Attitude and helpfulness of staff and practitioners
- Collaboration between staff in delivery of care
- Consistency and frequency of staff practicing service excellence behaviors
- Timely responsiveness to patient's needs, questions, concerns

Communication:

- Pre- and Post- Appointment communication, follow-up, and reminders
- Communication effectiveness between staff and clinicians
- Explaining procedures in advance before and during appointment
- Managing time expectations—communicating proactively, and responsive in the face of delays, or anticipated delays
- Clinical treatment explained fully, and patient's questions answered

Patient Chairside:

- Ability to quickly build rapport and establish credibility/ trust with patient
- Confirming patient understands treatment and care plans
- Solicit input and collaboration from patient on their treatment and care
- Spend adequate time with patient (no rushed appointments)

Cleanliness (especially since onset of Covid-19):

- Availability and accessibility of sanitizing products
- Overall condition of cleanliness of walls, floors, furniture, operatory
- The absence of unpleasant odors

Ease of Appointment Scheduling:

- Online appointment booking, one click, live chat, FAQs answered
- Speed/ease of new patient intake online (paperless process)
- Computer and mobile-friendly access
- Text and email reminders and follow-up

Building a Culture of Service Excellence

The widely accepted best practice cornerstones to build a company culture of service excellence are:

- Effective senior leaders/owners continually practicing and reinforcing service excellence behaviors themselves.
- Commitment to service excellence and patient experience/satisfaction being a cornerstone to daily operations and business results.
- Creation of behavior standards linked to company goals, service excellence, and the patient experience.
- Employee engagement is a priority, especially soliciting their input, involving them in problem-solving and engaging them in solutions.
- Recognition and reward for quick wins, progress, and people's contributions.
- Creation of a high accountability culture, both individually and collectively.
- Consistent frequent effective communication throughout the entire organization.

PROVIDING INDIVIDUALIZED CARE AND TREATMENT

In previous chapters in the sections, *Your People* and *Your Patients,* we provided specific tactics, tools and strategies that positively impact your team members' experiences which in turn impact your patient experience. The rest of this chapter provides proven best practices, from inside and outside Dentistry, in the following areas:

1. Language and Scripting
2. Inside Your Practice
3. Service Excellence Delivery
4. Personalized Patient Experience

These are numbered 1 through 4 because the order in which you address these is important. Language and scripting are foundational to creating a culture of service excellence. Many of the companies ranked in the top 20 of Fortune's *Best Companies to Work for* List credit language and scripting as being core to their success in building a lasting culture of excellence for their employees and their customers.

> The ROI for investing in, and implementing these best practices, is improving the patient experience in terms of the top five patient satisfaction drivers—service delivery, communication, chairside interaction, cleanliness, and appointment scheduling.

1. LANGUAGE AND SCRIPTING

The 3 O'clock Parade

During new hire orientation, Walt Disney World Cast Members learn the most asked Guest question inside the Magic Kingdom Theme Park is,

"What time is the 3 o'clock parade?"

The afternoon parade with Disney characters in the Magic Kingdom begins at 3pm EST every day of the year. Yet the *magic* of Disney Guest service training teaches something far more important than just the answer to this question. Disney teaches their Cast to listen for the ***question behind the question***. It turns out the real questions Magic Kingdom Guests are asking are, "When does the 3 o'clock parade get to where I am standing now?" "Where is the best place to see the parade?" or "How far ahead of time do I need to find a seat along the parade route?"

The *magical* Guest service responses may be "3:05 or 3:20," depending in what *Land* the Guest is standing; or "Standing upstairs at the Walt Disney World Train station has a great view," or "The good news is our characters are now performing on floats much higher in the air, so you no longer have to worry about getting a *great seat* on the curb along the parade route by 2pm."

Delivering this *magical* level of Guest service requires:

- Knowing and understanding the Guests' needs, expectations, and desires
- Curating all possible *best answers* to Guest questions, including the questions Guests don't know to ask because it is their first visit
- Training your staff to fully understand the Guest experience, and the questions that may arise, including the *questions behind the question*
- Providing staff with the language or key words to use in their responses

Translating *Disney* to Dental

Let's translate this to a new Dental patient experience. When a patient is confirming the date and time of their first appointment, what are all the possible questions this new patient may have?

- How long does it take to get from my home to the dental office coming from the North…from the South…from the West…from downtown, etc.?

- Is it better to come to I-95 to get to you, or to take 276 instead? Is there a way to get there that avoids highways and toll roads?
- Is there any road construction you know of right now that will cause a delay?
- Where is the parking lot, or how far away is parking from the office?
- Is parking free or is there a charge? Can I get paid parking validated?
- If street parking, does it take quarters or only accept payment through a mobile app?
- Are Lyft and Uber drivers readily available around your office? Since my spouse is out of town, and I am receiving IV sedation for my treatment, may I arrive and leave via Lyft and Uber drivers?
- With Covid, do I have to stay outside and call you first, before coming into the office? Are masks still required? Can my spouse come inside the office with me for my appointment?
- Which entrance of the building, specifically, do I park closest to (medical office complex)?
- Where is the best handicap parking for me to use?
- What happens on a *snow day*? How do I find out if the office is open?
- I'm a single parent, and my appointment is after school hours. Can I bring a small child with me to the appointment? Do you have a child-friendly waiting area?
- Is public transportation feasible to get to your office? Local train—which stop is best?

Now consider...

For how many of these questions do you have complete answers printed and available on every office phone which could be used for a new patient conversation? Or accessible online from every telephone?

So many of these questions are important, yet your patient doesn't know what they don't know; they have never been to your office; and therefore, they don't know the questions they could or should be asking.

Service excellence and creating a great patient experience are achieved when you and your team have this process mapped out, with all pertinent information available for staff, and you conduct continuous training on delivering service excellence.

More to consider...

- Do you have team members who are fluent in the other languages of your patients? Do you have fluent speakers of other languages every day of the week?

- Do you have pages on your website already translated into the most common foreign languages used by your patients? (*Bablic* is one trusted resource for a multi-language website– of course, Google browser provides translation)

- If your dental practice closes its office from 12pm to 1pm every day, does your call center or answering service still answer your phones live during this one hour?

According to a few industry surveys, the two most common roadblocks causing your new patients to cancel or "no show" their first appointment are 1) difficulty reaching the office, 2) poor quality reviews online (average rating less than 4 stars).

The Ten Most Commonly Asked Patient Questions

As mentioned earlier, whether you use online solutions or printed pages, have the answers to at least the ten most asked patient questions available at every phone which will be used for patient conversations.

This may include call centers, front desk, lab, business offices, after hours service, and hygiene or operatory support stations. Have a single page on your site dedicated to directions and navigating to the office. For example, www.XYZdental.com/directions. This way anyone can share this link during a conversation, on a voicemail, or in an email or text message.

The key distinction here in providing service excellence is your commitment to anticipating the needs of your patients in all aspects of the patient experience.

"I Don't Know." versus "That's a Great Question..."

Another Disney best practice and service standard to be followed by all Disney Cast Members worldwide, is to never respond to a Guest question with "I don't know." Instead, the more graceful service excellence response is "That's a great question." This statement is then followed immediately by either "May I take a moment to find the answer for you?" or something like, "Let me check on this (research this) and get right back to you. Is this the best number to reach you (e.g., confirm their cell number)?" "Will you be available to receive a call in the next 30 to 60 minutes?"

"If you were my brother, sister, father, or mother..."

Over the years, Dr. Sean has found the following dialogue to result in increased case acceptance, an increase in the patient's trust in Dr. Sean, and a greater sense of certainty and confidence in the decision by the patient, and greater patient satisfaction.

When reviewing various treatment and care options with a patient, Dr. Sean oftentimes proactively offers some form of this statement—"If you were my (brother, sister, father or mother), this is the "XYZ"

I would choose for you. This would be the best treatment, yet obviously you have these other choices too."

Dr. Sean's intention here is rooted in his belief that his role is to provide his patients with the information necessary for them to make the most informed decision possible.

"I chose Dr. Sean because he was so confident he could transform my smile!"
—Samer Saah

"My self-esteem was dwindling, and I was so worried about what others thought or said about me when they saw me. I always smiled with my mouth closed. People would even make nasty comments to me. I had seen multiple dentists, but they were all too pushy and salesy, and seemed to only care about the money, not me, the patient.

Dr. Sean was the opposite. He and his team made it easy breezy for me and made me so comfortable every step of the way. Dr. Sean is the vanguard of this procedure. His confidence and certainty he could help me reduced my anxiety and worry.

Now I have no sensitive teeth, I smile with confidence, and I no longer worry about what others are thinking about me. Your smile is the gateway to your soul, and this procedure is an investment in your new life! Dr. Sean is truly a hero, with magic hands, a huge heart, and the Midas touch!"

Answer the *Why* and Share the *Because*

As discussed in the chapters, *The Power of Connecting and Converting Patients Over the Phone,* and *Case Acceptance: Think Treatment Conversations*, whenever possible, answer the *Why Questions* for your patients. Answering the *Why* for patients builds trust, and often gives them more confidence in choosing you as their dentist, because of the well-informed decisions they made regarding their treatment plan.

Borrowing from the proven methods of *NLP*, when either making a request of someone else, or when answering the *Why Question*, be sure to use the word "because" in your sentence. The simple yet powerful use of "because" results in far greater acceptance or adoption of your communication. One study showed that when a gentleman approached a stranger on a public sidewalk simply asking, "May I borrow your cell phone?" versus "May I borrow your cellphone to make a call because my phone is dead?" The number of times strangers agreed and offered their phone for the man's use (almost instantly) when he included "…because my phone is dead?" was exponentially higher than when he did not use the "because" phrase.

2. INSIDE YOUR PRACTICE

The following are best practices to use inside your practice as part of building your company culture of service excellence. The big question here is whether your practice can handle these enhancements in terms of staffing, scheduling, profitability, service, and demand on other resources. It is also important to be sure you are implementing new enhancements which are valued by your patients. This reinforces the importance of hosting patient focus groups at least once a year to listen and discover what your patients truly want. For any of these items which you may already have in practice, simply check in with your staff to see if they are being consistently practiced.

Loyalty Plan

Concierge doctors and dental plans are continuing to grow. For dentists, the concierge or loyalty plans include no deductibles, no yearly maximum, no waiting periods, fixed annual fees for children, adults and periodontal (e.g., $150/yr.; $250/yr.; $350/yr.). Weekend and evening hours are included by some practices, e.g., 8am to 2pm on Saturday; 7am opening twice a week; open until 8pm twice a week with discounted rates for treatments included.

An example of services offered in one year, by a general dentist:

- Children: two professional cleanings; two regular exams; two fluoride treatments; one-time radiographs
- Adults: two professional cleanings; two regular exams; two oral screenings; one-time radiographs
- Periodontal: two regular exams; three maintenance cleanings; two oral screenings; one-time radiographs

This model is still positioning general dentistry as a commodity service, and you are competing on price. However, some of these adjustments may help with acquiring new patients, enhancing patient satisfaction, or create a competitive advantage in your market.

Dentist Arrival

The dentist arrives 30 minutes prior to the first appointment. This enables the dentist to have five-minute huddles, check-in with select staff, solicit input from staff on improvements, and other priorities.

Office Closed

If you close your office every day between 12pm and 1pm, at least have your answering service, call center, or staff member answer incoming calls live during this hour. Remember, ease of appointment scheduling and changes is one of the top five patient satisfaction drivers.

Insurance Concierge

Designating a single team member to be the patient liaison regarding everything insurance-related is great for patient satisfaction. Yet scaling this staffing wise is sometimes cost prohibitive.

Soothing Spa Features

Believe it or not, more than just pediatric practices are utilizing therapy/companion dogs, aquariums, water features, aromatherapy, adjustable lighting in the waiting room, and even a quiet chair section in the patient waiting room.

Mobile Friendly Website

According to multiple market studies in dentistry, as much as 60% of your patients and prospective patients are looking at your website on their phone or other mobile devices. This is especially true for your patients under the age of 40. Remember, service, communication and appointment scheduling are three of the top five patient satisfaction drivers. Be sure to check on your current website(s) for mobile-friendly user experience.

Post-Visit Feedback Surveys

Thriving growing practices have systems in place to automate the outreach and collection of post-visit feedback from patients. The key is to ask the right questions in your survey. There are several validated free tools online for creating your survey.

Online Reviews

Especially for patients under 45, online reviews have a significant influence in selecting a new dentist, for about 30%-40% of your patients, according to multiple recent surveys. For disgruntled reviewers, offering a clear and simple way for them to contact you, e.g., email address or texting number listed in your response.

Be sure to reply to positive and negative reviews. Always reply to online reviews first by thanking the reviewer for their feedback, using language such as "Thank you for your feedback. Your feedback is valuable so we may continue to improve our patient experience."

Ceiling in Operatory

Inspired by successful use in hospitals, some dental practices install quotes, inspirational messages, or images on the ceiling directly above each patient chair. This may have a calming effect or a form of distraction for your more anxious, nervous or scared patients.

Office Furnishings

Quite often dental practices go far too long, oftentimes several years, without updating their patient's waiting room, or hallways. Everything from steam cleaning sofa fabric, sanitizing surfaces, replacing old artwork, updating furniture, or even painting the walls a brighter different color are simple yet important updates to be made.

Automated Delivery of Notecards

Patients and staff appreciate receiving a note at home from you, especially if your message is personalized or specific. There are several companies available who print, sign and mail personalized notecards. In terms of your staff, don't be surprised when you find out one of your team member's young children took your thank you note to school for show and tell. Truly this happens more often than you may think.

Pre- and/or Post-shift Team Huddles

Conducting a structured yet informal *5-minute huddle* with your team at the beginning or end of the day is a proven best practice in hospitals for improving employee engagement, interdepartmental communication, and patient satisfaction. Typically, only three items are on the agenda, and one is a reminder of a specific service excellence behavior standard or celebration of ways a team member provided exceptional service to a patient. These huddles are best held without food or drink, with all attendees standing.

Timely Team Feedback

This $30 solution is one of the simplest yet most powerful tools for improving team and interdepartmental communication, and reducing if not eliminating miscommunication, misunderstanding, or poor service delivery. Installing a 3M Post-it® Flip Chart on a wall in an employee-only area that is convenient for all employees to see, is a great team communication and "pass-on log" tool. Throughout the day, your team members may go to the board and write down a situation, scenario, issue, problem, challenge, or simply an update that is important for almost all or all team members to be aware of and/or discuss. This list can be addressed at 5-minute huddles at the end of the day or first thing in the morning. Some examples of topics to have on your flipchart page are:

- Updates
- Stop, Start, Continue—staff suggesting something we need to stop, start, or continue doing for the team or for patients
- Discovery—anything new that most or all staff need to be aware of, e.g., half of the front parking lot is being re-paved Tuesday and Wednesday, so no parking there from 8am Tuesday until 8am Thursday.

Disney's Tele-Cast

Years ago, every day at Walt Disney World theme parks, Cast Members (employees) were given a trifold, double-sided, pocket-sized information card which listed all relevant show times, theme park hours, telephone numbers, Guest information, and unique information relevant to *this week* which is most useful in answering Guests' questions. Depending on the size of your dental practice, you may not need to distribute these cards to every team member, and instead, have the information posted in a few employee areas throughout your practice. Today, you may replace this printed card with an app.

Disney's Backstage Mirrors

In Cast Member locker rooms and on the wall next to any doors that open to an onstage area (Guest area), there are 3' x 5' mirrors so Cast Members can check their costume and appearance before stepping on stage. The placement of the mirror directly next to the doorway, or on the door, ensures most staff will pause to check their appearance before returning to patient areas.

Team Members... Dressed to Impress

Your staff's appearance says a lot when they interact with your patients. When onboarding new hires, and periodically, as a reminder to all staff, be sure to teach the importance of maintaining professional attire and appearance. This includes consistent hygiene, hair care, makeup, and odor control (e.g., vaping, smoking), and clothes and/or uniforms kept clean and wrinkle-free. Walt Disney World has candy-type vending machines backstage providing Cast Members grooming, hygiene, and hair care products, such as hair bands, pins, combs, brushes, feminine products, razors, shampoo, conditioner, and shaving cream. Cast Members purchase these products with deeply discounted prices.

3. SERVICE EXCELLENCE DELIVERY

IV Sedation

There are several benefits of using IV sedation:

- less stress, anxiety, pain, discomfort for patients
- patient's memory of treatment is minimized

- more pleasant patient experience
- reduces gag reflex and lessens patient movement during treatment
- enables more treatments to be completed in fewer visits
- makes longer appointments for treatments possible

Seal the Deal Calls: Pre-Visit New Patient Phone Calls

Steve Sperry, of *Inventive Dental Solutions* teaches *Seal the Deal Calls.* These are phone calls made to new patients prior to their first visit. The Dentist or Associate Dentist says "Thank you for choosing us for your dental home/family. My name is Dr. _____ and I make a point of reaching out to all my new patients to introduce myself." Another sentence showcasing the unique aspect of the patient experience may be included here as well.

Post-Visit Patient Phone Calls

Calling every patient, the next day after their office visit or treatments is a proven best practice with value that cannot be overstated. The best practices are to:

- Contact at least 60% of each day's patients
- Have clinical staff make the patient phone calls so patients' questions are more likely to be answered immediately on this call
- Owners and dentists should strive to complete two or three patient calls themselves each day, or at a minimum leave a meaningful thoughtful voice mail for the patient if they do not answer the call
- Some practices incorporate one or two post-visit survey questions into their phone call script as well

Online Appointment Booking and Payments

With the vast number of hospitals and medical groups or systems which have successfully implemented interactive online patient portals including the convenience of a patient portal app, many more dental patients now expect to have a patient portal. Patients want to schedule, reschedule or cancel appointments online, pay their bills, check insurance claims, and access their dental records.

This best practice enhances patient satisfaction, improves efficiency for the practice, and optimizes appointment scheduling. Another appointment scheduling best practice is to book the patient's next appointment (e.g., hygiene or routine), and collect any payments as well, when the patient first arrives and checks in at reception. This enables patients to leave quickly after their appointment ends. This has been shown to improve patient satisfaction and patient throughput efficiency. Especially during Covid, and after, more and more patients appreciate contactless payment options. Younger patients even prefer it. Additionally, this method tends to result in a greater collection rate for patients' copayments and current balances.

Some other significant benefits from the use of a patient portal are the reduction in cancellations, boosting efficiencies and daily production. Reportedly, more than 90% of the most profitable dental practices are using technology to automate communication with patients as well. Apparently most dental patients would like to communicate with the practice and schedule appointments from the dentist's Google business profile too.

Wayfinding

Now a standard for service excellence in hospitals, *Wayfinding* is a major patient satisfaction driver. *Wayfinding* includes everything from providing driving directions to your practice; directional signage in the parking lot and in the building; navigating the office;

and the arrival process for appointments; and the exit after the appointment. Excellent wayfinding includes the same information to another dental practice or specialist to whom you are referring your patient. As I mentioned before, I discovered offering IV Sedation and offering more treatment procedures reduces the number of other dentists our patients must see.

Debit/Credit Card Decline

A patient may get embarrassed when their form of payment is declined. Using diplomatic graceful language at this moment minimizes the awkward silence or patient's embarrassment. Some key words to consider using are:

- I apologize for the inconvenience; ...would you please swipe your card one more time. Or you may say, ...may I attempt to scan the card one more time?
- I apologize, our system sometimes does this. Please try swiping your card one more time. (Most of the time, your patient knows why their card was declined and simply provide a separate form of payment)
- Depending on your practice's policy, you may empower your staff to offer an "IOU" letting the patient pay later. Obviously, this increases outstanding receivables, so this offer requires discernment.

New Patients

Like onboarding new hires, first impressions and the initial patient experience for new patients are critical to patient satisfaction and patients returning for future appointments. This also contributes to the likelihood of a satisfied patient writing a positive review and/or bringing family members or referring others to your practice. Most dental practices provide a new patient with the traditional "gift bag" of free items and perhaps a coffee mug with the practice logo.

To enhance your new patient welcome gift consider providing the following:

- Extra brand chewing gum, approved for use with braces
- Toothbrush holder or water rinsing cup for their bathroom
- Discount voucher for a cordless, rechargeable water flosser, or electric toothbrush
- Complimentary voucher for facial and manicure at a local spa, for full-arch patients
- Rechargeable facial cleansing brush

The Disney distinction is to provide items which are in line with your patient's experience within your practice. For example, what would a patient appreciate the most after receiving a full arch replacement?

"I was referred to Dr. Sean by staff from a competing dental practice!"
—Arnulfo Puentes

"I've struggled with my teeth for many years, with difficult issues with my molars, working with multiple dentists, and my teeth deteriorating. When my wife and I were visiting a dental practice for an initial consultation, the receptionist overheard our conversation and referred us to Dr. Sean! Everything changed after working with Dr. Sean. I began to smile again, my appearance, and even my grooming improved. Now I have far less visits to my dentist, and I'm pain free.

In my career in aerospace, I have seen a lot of great customer service. Working with Dr. Sean and his team was amazing, exceptional at every level, at every step. The people, the process, the setup, the procedure, the patient care, and the follow up, are all world class!"

4. PERSONALIZED PATIENT EXPERIENCE

Every patient is unique, with different expectations, concerns, fears, and desires. Our team takes pride in being able to provide the most personalized patient experience, tailored to each patient's needs. This can be a daunting task at times, however, there are proven best practices worth considering for your own practice.

The Five Minutes that Change Everything

In the first chapter of the *Your Patients* section, entitled *Did You Hear Me? Empathic Listening,* I shared the list of what I do in the first five minutes of every patient appointment–***The Magic Five***. The key to this most important best practice is to focus on being fully present with my patient, with the intention for a great patient interaction, and investing the time to actively listen to them. In those first five minutes, I want my patients to genuinely feel they are the single most important person in the world to me. This intense focus helps me transition between patients more calmly as well.

Personal Note in Patient's Record

Like teaching your people how to listen for the *question behind the question* (What time is the 3 o'clock parade?), teach your team members how to ask questions of patients, and how to listen for personal notes to enter into the patient's record. It's important to use one of these notes in a patient conversation to build rapport and trust. Patients are impressed and possibly moved or touched emotionally when you or your team members remember one of these notes at the patient's next appointment. Be sure to train your staff where to put these notes in your patient record system.

- Examples of personal notes worth jotting down in a patient's record may be:
- Patient's preferred name, and how to properly pronounce it

- Birthday, special events, e.g., family, vacation, graduation, heading to college
- Pets' names and type of pet—Butterscotch, their Goldendoodle
- Sports or hobby interests—golf, their favorite pro sports team, or painting and pottery
- Important milestones coming up—retirement, wedding, anniversary

Comfort Closets

Providing various personal items for patients goes a long way in increasing patient satisfaction. Create a storage space/closet which holds comfort closet items such as:

- neck pillow, soothing lip balm, eye masks
- stress balls, weighted blanket, noise-canceling headphones (allow Bluetooth earbuds during hygiene appts)
- disposable ear plugs, and disposable tinted glasses
- face masks and hand sanitizer may be the norm for years to come

Communicating with Patients the Day of Their Appointment

Many practices use automated messaging services—voicemail and text messaging—which are great enhancements. However, one best practice for communicating with patients on the day of their appointment is to *manually* send a text message to the patient with a brief personal note. Sending these messages out can help you answer questions or address concerns before the patient arrives for their appointment.

Personalized Patient Videos

There are now several video recording platforms and browser plug-ins which enable you, your Associates, or your staff to record a brief personalized video message which is sent to the patient by email using one of these platform services. Your patients will greatly appreciate the time you invested to shoot a quick personal video message just for them. Sending these personalized videos by email to your team members is also a way to increase communications with individual team members.

Some dental practices have recorded short *meet-n-greet* or *introduction*-type videos showcasing the dentists and key staff with direct patient interaction. These quick videos also work well on your practice website, e.g., on the *About* or *Who We Are* page of your website.

Behavioral Styles Training

One of the most transformational skills building training you can offer your team members is behavioral styles (personality) training. This training helps team members understand themselves, one another, their boss, and their patients. Specifically understanding what each of the four styles value, except for others, and how they prefer to be communicated with in various scenarios. In the resource section of our website, you can download a list of behavioral styles training providers. You may have heard of DiSC, Platinum Rule, MyersBriggs.

New Patient Office Tour

In this mobile-friendly digital age, dental practices are posting walk-through videos of their practice on their website, in addition to providing in person office tours. During the walk-through video, you may wish to have a key player from each department appear on camera to welcome new patients to your practice.

For some more great examples and insights from the Walt Disney World company and Disney Institute, simply download the *What is the Disney Difference? Guide,* from Steven Rowell's book, *Success from the Inside Out.*

Chapter 14
REFLECTION:
Achieving Service Excellence: Fostering a Culture of Quality Outcomes

1. Which one of the five drivers of patient satisfaction is the greatest opportunity for improvement in my practice(s)?

   Service, Communication, Chairside,
   Cleanliness, Appt Scheduling

2. As an owner, what specific behaviors can I practice consistently to be a better role model of service excellence?

3. Which of the four cornerstones is the best place to start to improve our service excellence and the patient experience?

   1. Language and Key Words
   2. Inside Your Practice
   3. Service Excellence Delivery
   4. Personalized Patient Experience

4. Thinking of the ***3 o'clock parade*** example and listening for the ***question behind the question,*** what are some of the most common questions patients ask my team members? What are the *questions behind the question* the patient is thinking but **not** asking?

5. Based on the cornerstone you chose above in #3, what would make the most **immediate** improvement in patient satisfaction? Which would provide the greatest **long-term** impact or improvement?

6. How am I doing with the first five minutes of my new patient appointments as it relates to creating a great patient experience? What are my Associates doing?

Chapter 14
ACTION:
Achieving Service Excellence: Fostering a Culture of Quality Outcomes

1. Ask your team which one of the five drivers of patient satisfaction is your greatest opportunity for improvement? Invite a small group of team members to brainstorm specific improvements and present their suggestions.

2. How could you implement the best practice (instead of saying, "I don't know.") of responding to a patient, guest, or family member with,

   "That's a great question. Let me find out for you and get right back to you" or, "That's a great question. May I take a moment to find the answer for you?"

3. Ask your team how consistently post-visit patient phone calls are being made? Address any deficiency or opportunities to improve.

4. Invite select team members to work in pairs to read the list of best practices in their category and suggest improvements. Give each pair one of these categories to work with and provide their suggestions:

   - Language and Key Words
   - Inside Your Practice
   - Service Excellence Delivery
   - Personalized Patient Experience

5. Identify the one best practice you will help your team implement over the next 30 days. Then enroll select staff

in the small task force which will lead the implementation of this one best practice over the next 30 days.

The following tools are available here:
www.TheresNoStandingStill.com

The What Is the Disney Difference? chapter from the book, Success from the Inside Out

Service Excellence Internal Assessment and Checklist

Your Practice

CHAPTER 15

Discover the Benefits of Implant Dentistry

"Implant dentistry is a must. It's the future. Over 60 million Americans are fully edentulous and over 100 million are partially edentulous."

When I got out of dental school, I wanted to be a cosmetic dentist who does the most beautiful crowns and fillings. That's what the focus of dental school is all about. How to have perfect margins and how to save every single tooth that we possibly can.

In 2005, at my Las Vegas practice, we were doing lots of cosmetic cases and veneers. Casino workers were making lots of cash at the time and could afford the $15,000 procedures. But then the economy crashed, and our cosmetic cases went down 80+% in just months. I was faced with a business-driven reality. It was almost like starting my practice all over again.

At this same time, I needed an implant myself. I went to a periodontist and the implant procedure only took 30 minutes. My procedures took 4 and 5 hours each. Intrigued by this experience, I realized general dentistry was no longer enough for me. I also realized I am a sucker for knowledge. I can't stop learning. Dental school provided me no surgical or dental implant experience. So, I started learning advanced cosmetic dentistry, orthodontics, neuromuscular dentistry, and earned my IV sedation license.

It took two-and-a-half years to transition to implant dentistry. I invested more than $30,000 in courses and wasn't making money for this two-and-a-half-year period. I completed a one-year residency at Loma Linda Dental School. I attended school for 4 days every six weeks, for an entire year. It was a 3-year journey to learn and become proficient in the All-on-4 implant procedures. What took me 5 years to learn, can now be learned in one year. Today, at 4M Institute, with the full arch dental implant course teaching the All-on-4 procedure, you can learn in 3 days, what took me 3 years to learn.

IV Sedation Changed My Life

During dental school I hated blood, in fact, if I saw blood I would faint. Yet when I discovered implant dentistry it stole my heart. I realized how straightforward surgery is and how gratifying it is to replace a tooth in fifteen minutes. It doesn't have to be bloody with today's technology. We get to do guided surgery. Obviously in full arch cases you get to see some blood. Nonetheless, I've loved implant dentistry ever since.

Getting my sedation license changed my life as well. Now I can perform so many different clinical procedures. When a patient comes to me, I am certain I can help them. I no longer refer my patients to multiple dentists and doctors. Instead, we provide multiple procedures all in one practice.

I hear so many dentists complaining there is so much competition out there; every dentist is doing whitening; every other dentist is doing Invisalign or aligners. Some dentists even call themselves cosmetic dentists. So, if you want to stand out you must do something different than all the other dentists.

After years of performing restorative dentistry, I discovered the All-on-4 dental implant technique. I saw firsthand the remarkable change, both emotional and physical, that this procedure has in my patients. I fell in love with the process. It has changed my life and daily it changes every patient's life in our offices.

The Innovation of Implant Dentistry

In 1971, a new airline, Southwest Airlines, started as an intrastate airline throughout Texas. They saw and seized the opportunity to provide short-hop flights between the many cities of Texas. At the time, there were millions of Texans who did not want to fly, for business or pleasure travel, preferring to drive. They saw air travel as expensive, time consuming, stressful, and buying tickets was complicated, and cancellations were costly. Put simply, travelers, especially business travelers, would rather drive themselves than fly.

Southwest changed the lives of Texans, especially business travelers, by offering more efficient, more convenient, and lower cost air travel. Southwest accomplished this by focusing on innovative logistics solutions, and using only one type of plane, the Boeing 737. They began providing a great customer experience, and being far easier to work with, especially with cancellations and airfare credits. They changed the airline industry by providing something that had never been offered before. They did all of this by recruiting and retaining motivated team members who enjoyed taking care of guests.

Like Southwest's pioneering innovation in the industry of air travel, Full Arch Implant dentistry, "teeth in a day," provides life changing dental care to millions of people who have suffered quietly for years, who:

- Don't know about their dental care options.
- Don't want the hassle and can't afford a bunch of different appointments, root canals, cleaning appointments.
- Don't have a lot of bone.

- Are suffering chronic pain with missing or rotting teeth.
- Don't want to go through sinus lift and six months of healing.
- Don't want to spend $70,000 or more on their mouth.
- Are afraid of dentists and dental work.
- Want quick results—want to walk out with healthy fixed teeth in one day.

Even though the All-On-4® (Paulo Malo, inventor) procedure began in 2000, and became more well known by 2012, this is still a huge "untapped market" in most cities.

What is Full Arch Implant Surgery?

The Full Arch Implant surgical procedure is when we place four implants in an edentulous arch (no teeth) to support a complete prosthesis. The front two implants are placed straight forward and straight up and down. The back two implants are tilted posteriorly or distally to where we can skip the sinus. We use very long implants so we can maximize the amount of bone that is there. The anterior part of the implant is more anterior to the jaw because this is the strongest part of the bone. As we go further back into the jaw the bone gets softer, especially in the upper arch. We tilt those implants so we can anchor to the better bone more anteriorly and yet the posterior part of the implant will be further back distally, which gives us a nice anterior posterior spread for a nice prosthetics to be restored.

The Full Arch Implant is a fixed prosthesis completed in one day. The patient walks in with no teeth or with teeth that need to be removed, and leaves with a fixed prosthesis the same day. This Full Arch Implant is also called "teeth in a day" or "all done in one day."

How big is the dental implant market share?

The ADA cites that dental implants are among the most significant advances in dentistry over the past 40 years. More and more dental patients are electing dental implants over crowns and bridges, because of the increase in comfort, speech improvement, and overall appearance. It has been projected that there are more than 150 million US citizens who are missing at least one tooth.

According to Fortune Business Insights, April 4, 2023, the market size of implant dentistry will be $4.4 billion in 2023 and is projected to reach $6.9 billion by 2030.

The NIH reported the prevalence of dental implants (estimated) to be 0.7% in 2000, with an increase to 5.7% in 2016. The NHI study projected the prevalence of tooth implants will continue to rise to 23% by 2026.

Why are dental implants so popular today?

Overall, implant dentistry offers numerous benefits that make it an ideal choice for people looking to replace missing teeth. Compared with traditional dentures and bridges, implants are extremely durable, much easier to clean and maintain, more comfortable to wear, and reduce dental pain. Implant dentistry has been shown to improve the quality of life for those who choose it. Not only does implant dentistry allow for a more natural appearance and better overall oral health, but it also allows patients to eat and speak with confidence. Implants can typically last for decades with proper care and maintenance. The success rate with implants is 95% to 98% depending on which study you reference. With all these benefits, implant dentistry continues to get even more popular year after year.

"From miserable to magical all in one day!"
—Glenn and Debbie Bernard

"We are one of those rare couples who both had the All on 4 procedures done, replacing all our teeth. My husband had only 5 teeth left, with dentures and bridges. He was miserable. I had 3 sets of crowns, and after bone loss, could have no more crowns. Then our next-door neighbors, a couple who both had full implants by Dr. Sean, told us we had to see him. At ages 80 and 67, the All on 4 procedures were life changing for us both! Glenn and I were in tears after looking in the mirror. Our only regret is that we didn't do it sooner.

For five years now, we have enjoyed eating, and smiling, with no pain. We referred our dog sitter and a dear friend from North Carolina to Dr. Sean. Dr. Sean cares about you as a person, and the way you feel. You are not just a number or a financial transaction. He truly wants you to be happy!"

How has Implantology changed over the past decade?

The actual surgical procedure part hasn't really changed much except refinements in technique. The instrumentation and technology used in the procedure has improved and evolved immensely to the point we have 100% guided surgery. CBCT surgical guides have made placing an implant far easier and require less surgical skills than back in 2000.

The most important improvements are in the design and materials of the prosthetics. Originally a patient's arch was replaced with a bar and dentures. The two major products being used for the final teeth are titanium bar with denture teeth, or full zirconia bridges. Each has advantages and disadvantages.

The titanium bar with denture teeth is lightweight, but not strong enough, so after a year or two, several teeth keep popping up or breaking off, requiring several repairs. The advantage for full zirconia is that it doesn't break that easily, yet the bridge is heavy, and screwed into four implants. There is a lot of wear and tear that occurs with such heavy zirconia. When the patient talks or chews, there can be a loud noise. Zirconia is too heavy, and it wears down the implants too quickly.

At 4M Implant Dental Center we took advantage of the lightness and flexibility of the denture teeth, and the strength and the aesthetic of the zirconium teeth. We use a material called Zirpeek, which has the strength of zirconia, yet is lightweight. We do individual crowns so if for some reason, one crown breaks, we can replace just the one crown as if it were a crown prep.

IV Sedation

Most of our patients are IV sedated for the Full Arch Implant procedure. If a patient is medically compromised, we have two or three days each month when we perform anesthesiologist cases. We don't teach IV sedation at 4M Institute but there are many great courses available. The issue of IV sedation or anesthesiologist cases doesn't have to be the determining factor whether you do these Full Arch Implant cases or not. When I first started, I would do oral sedation for patients and just start with one arch. The procedure gets easier as you do more of them obviously. You do save a lot of time when you do IV sedation yourself or utilize an anesthesiologist.

Your Own Laboratory

We have our own laboratory in the 4M Dental Implant Center in Long Beach, so all our cases' lab work is conducted in house. We have tremendous cost savings compared to outsourced lab fees. We create our own prostheses with the breakthrough material Zirpeek. If you are building your practice to grow with implantology you need your own lab. It is critical to be able to duplicate things in a timely manner or provide the services required with the Full Arch Implant procedure.

Our Patients Are Not Wealthy Celebrities

Understandably for lots of reasons, there is a common misperception Full Arch Implants are only possible for wealthy people and celebrities. Most of our patients are blue-collar, hardworking men and women who haven't had proper dental care for 10, 20 or 30 years, whether it was due to finances, time, parents, fear of dentistry, or lack of knowledge. They have reached a point in their life in terms of dental health and hygiene where they are suffering significantly e.g., in their love life, occupation, career advancement, or it is impacting their physical health. Oftentimes they have suffered quietly with chronic pain and missing or rotting teeth.

Financing

More than 90% of our patients obtain third-party financing to cover the investment in their new smile and improved health. Most patients receive help from direct family or extended family members, either from direct financial support, or by way of co-signing the loan. Our patients, on average, invest $25,000 per arch for the Full Arch Implant procedure. There are several trustworthy third-party financing firms with whom our patients have worked. We are truly driven to change our patients' lives and therefore, in the event our patient is unable to obtain third-party financing for the entire procedure investment, we may be able to cover this through our *Bridge the Gap* financial support.

The Big Mistake Most Dentists Make

Not all dental practices are sitting in the posh luxury of Beverly Hills. Many of our patients are hardworking, honest, loyal, honorable blue-collar workers. One day we had a gentleman named Ben come in for an initial consultation. His appearance was disheveled, his body odor was pungent, and one could understandably assume he was homeless. Sometimes your staff's attitude toward this person may change, even just slightly. Your attitude may change too. Some short-sighted less compassionate dentists might think to themselves, "What is he doing here? Don't waste your time. He can't afford implants."

The big mistake most dentists make is when *they think for their patient and choose for their patient.* I did this myself for many years. To that point, I would never be where I am today if I had not learned this priceless lesson from one of my own mentors.

Be honest with yourself as you consider…

How many times when meeting a new patient, have you decided (made a snap judgment) "This person can't afford XYZ, so I'm going to offer a lower cost option." Yet you have no knowledge whether the patient can or cannot afford it.

We treated Ben with the same level of care and attention as all our patients, recognizing his urgent need for dental implants. The cost of this necessary treatment amounted to $40,000. Although Ben appreciated our thorough examination and consultation, he didn't make a firm commitment to the investment at the time. Uncertain if we would ever see him again, we were pleasantly surprised when, just two days later, Ben arrived with a paper grocery sack containing the exact amount in cash. His commitment to his dental health was truly remarkable.

I do not choose for my patients. Instead, after asking questions, actively listening, and fully examining the patient, I will share the available options, answer their questions, and let them choose. My job is to help them make the most informed decision possible.

Training is Key to Your Success

This one skill, IV Sedation, opened the door to offering multiple services within one practice. Throughout this book you have heard me discuss the transformational power of post-graduate education and skill building. The transformation is powerful, empowering, and equipping both personally and professionally.

Remember, competence breeds confidence. Confidence is what your patients are looking for when shopping for a dentist. Your confidence creates certainty in the patient's mind which leads to case acceptance.

"Pain free implants in one day...and they pulled 11 teeth!"
—Bob Downey

"After seeing five other implant doctors, at age 78, I toured Dr. Sean's Long Beach office, and I was sold on them right away. I had multiple bridges and only a few teeth showing before implant surgery. I was worried about my age, bone density, and whether I could handle the procedure. Dr. Sean's confidence after looking at my x-rays put me at ease, and his team is excellent in every way. I couldn't believe after only one day of surgery I had all my implants and teeth in place. I had no pain or discomfort, and didn't even need Tylenol afterwards, even though they pulled 11 teeth!

I mistakenly started taking my blood thinner medicine one day after surgery, and my gums began to bleed. Dr. Sean met me in his Anaheim office on a Sunday and patched me up immediately. What doctor does this for his patients? Dr. Sean is extraordinary!"

The answer is in the team! Getting your team members trained and onboard is critical. If your people don't know how to do a procedure, or your front desk staff don't know how to talk about it, and your marketing doesn't communicate it, you are going to be gravely disappointed. At 4M Institute, we offer Team Training–ETT Elite Team Training; Surgical Assistant Training; and Call Center Boot Camp Training.

Chapter 15
REFLECTION:
Discover the Benefits of Implant Dentistry

1. What is truly unique about my practice, the services we offer, or how we deliver our services? Do we have a competitive advantage?
2. (If not providing IV sedation) Why am I not providing this service? What is holding me back? Is now the time to add this to my practice?
3. How would my practice(s) grow if I had my own lab? Is this something to add to my strategic plan for next year?
4. (If not offering 3rd party financing) Is the reason I have always provided our own financing still valid today? Or should I look at 3rd party financing with fresh eyes? How would 3rd party financing help my practice grow or help my patients?
5. Do I make assumptions about my new patients, and therefore make snap judgments which change the way I offer treatment options? Do I "think for my patients and choose for them" rather than show them their options and let them make their own informed decision?
6. What is a new skill—clinical, operational, business, finance, leadership—I will learn over the next six months?

Chapter 15

ACTION:

Discover the Benefits of Implant Dentistry

1. What specifically can you do to begin no longer "assuming, thinking, and choosing" for your patients? How can you catch yourself, or prompt yourself to stop doing it during patient conversations?
2. Schedule time for yourself to take an honest inventory of your practice's competitive advantage and whether you are doing anything to stand out from the crowd in your local market.
3. Schedule time to research training/certification in IV sedation. Set a future date in your calendar as a target for when you will have completed this training.
4. Reach out to Dr. Sean for insights regarding the feasibility of adding your own in- house Lab.
5. Schedule an appointment on your calendar to research 3rd party financing options for your practice(s).
6. Schedule an appointment on your calendar to research options for your new training class/course/program to learn a new skill. Write a declaration statement to someone to inspire you to follow through on this. For example, send an email to your business coach or accountability partner stating, "By September 2023, I will be enrolled in XYZ training course, with a goal for completion before May 2024. Obtaining this new skill will enable me to __________________."
7. Ask your team leaders and members for training ideas for them as well.

CHAPTER 16

Employee Engagement: The Key to Success

"Little hinges swing big doors."
—W. Clement Stone

Throughout this book, such as in the chapters *The Power of Influence,* and *Retaining Valuable Team Members* you have discovered or rediscovered many ways leaders establish their credibility and influence, build trust with others, invest in the growth of their people and themselves, and build high performing teams.

Employee engagement has been a top priority for employers nationwide who want to retain their people by providing meaningful work, great communication, valuing their contributions, asking for their input, and providing them feedback. Great employers consistently maintain open dialogue with their people, ensure their vision is clearly understood, and routinely share their expectations and the "why" behind what they expect and what they do.

There are thousands of leadership books with hundreds of them focused on how to improve employee engagement, with the promises of boosting productivity, profitability, performance, and retention, to name just a few.

However, far too often, we make things more complicated than they need to be.

Effective employee engagement comes down to the most fundamental issue at work—trusting relationships. From your team members' perspective, it is "all about" trust, fairness, consistency, communication, involvement, dignity, respect, and being valued for their contributions.

My first dental practice started in Las Vegas. It is still running today. As you know, owning and operating only one dental practice location, you are there every day, as the owner and the leader. Your people tend to learn what you expect of them over time, and because you are there every day, you can address any concerns you or they may have.

However, as I began growing our practice into multiple offices in California, I could no longer be in Las Vegas as much or as often. One concern I spent lots of time thinking about is "What will happen to my original practice, now that I am not there as often?"

Over the next two years, I flew back and forth between Las Vegas and Long Beach, many times. I paid a significant price for this in my marriage and as a father of three daughters. Over time, as we were opening our new locations, I learned the importance of new hire orientation, onboarding new hires, and ensuring everyone knew what was expected of them, and how they can succeed in their role, their team, and our practice overall, especially with our commitment to excellence and our patients.

We did this better in some locations than others. Then a couple years ago, I became concerned about what was happening at our Las Vegas practice, both for our people, and our patients. We were taking great care of our patients, yet turnover and human resource issues were growing. I had been spending 90%+ of my time in our California offices, and 4M Institute in Long Beach.

We scheduled a full-day team meeting in our Las Vegas practice to bring everyone together. We have done this before with varying degrees of success at all our locations. Yet this meeting was different. I wasn't sure it would work or have the impact we were hoping it would have, yet I trusted my coaches.

The following is the framework of this team meeting, which I used to reconnect our team members with one another, to connect with new staff myself, and to communicate our vision, values, mission, expectations, and goals with everyone in our Las Vegas practice.

I realized many of our newer staff didn't really know me, and this was a great opportunity to reconnect everyone to our mission.

With the help of Steven Rowell, we created the outline for this meeting, and especially, the message I delivered to our staff. I trusted the process yet honestly was not sure how it would be received. The results exceeded my expectations. After the meeting, some of my most longtime staff shared how they appreciated learning more about me as a person, not just as a *doctor owner*. They shared how reenergized they were after hearing the passion I have for excellence and taking care of our patients. Newer team members were inspired by getting to know their coworkers more, and appreciated learning about me, the history and mission of our practice, and to learn how they could contribute to our success.

We are now working to incorporate this same information into our new hire orientation, and into our opening activities for new locations. We can do this annually for each of our California locations as well. This interactive experience with your staff and associates gives you the opportunity to build trust with your team members, re-recruit your staff for retention, clarify definitions of success and excellence, communicate your expectations, and share what you, the owner, are willing to do in support of your team members. When you add the opportunity to get feedback from your staff as well, they feel heard and know their input and opinions matter. The energy from all this keeps your company culture "alive and real" for your staff and associates as well.

The Premise for This Team Meeting

The opportunity here is for you, the owner, to "humanize" yourself for your team's sake for the following reasons:

- Learn a little bit about you, your personal story, your values, and your definition of excellence
- Build trust with your team when they learn more about you and your expectations of them
- Build confidence in your informal group leaders amongst your team, and your top performing team members who already champion you and your mission
- Empower your leaders, informal group leaders, and top performers to speak up and reinforce your message, after the meeting, with any team members who may be negative or "not on the bus"
- Employee engagement, loyalty, and retention will increase for many of your team members
- Stress reduction for team members of all types due to the sharing of your personal story; values; beliefs; definition of excellence; definition of success; and expectations of yourself and them

Talking Points

For each of the following categories, choose 3 or 4 points which are most important to you, and/or the most important messages you want your team members to hear right now. When appropriate, share your expectations of yourself and your commitment to your team. This will take 15 to 30 minutes to present, depending upon how many stories you wish to tell along the way. Using presentation slides for each category with your bulleted lists is recommended, especially for your visual learners on your team.

Structure of Your Talk

This talk covers several topics and the order you present them in is extremely important. Be as vulnerable as you can in sharing because the more vulnerable you are, the greater trust is built. This presentation is designed to serve as a catalyst for your people and your business. It is not just some "warm fuzzy rah-rah session." Quite the opposite, it is a design informed by the major research and evidence-based outcomes in employee engagement today. For example, the topics covered in this meeting design and the experience improve the factors measured in Gallup's Q12 Engagement Survey.

My Personal Story

Begin your presentation here, being as vulnerable as possible. This humanizes you and builds trust with your team members. Obviously sharing the positive triumphs and successes in your life can be inspiring to some people. Yet it is far more impactful for you to share 1 or 2 failures or challenges you faced in your life, the lessons you learned, and how you overcame them, rather than *just* sharing positive outcomes and celebrations in your life.

Examples:

- As a young kid I always dreamed of becoming a ________ because...but then I had *"xyz"* experience and that changed everything
- My father teaching me the value of hard work and dedication
- Coming to America at 15, as a first-generation immigrant to the US, being bullied in school, and how this taught me perseverance
- Discovering a Mentor from ______ who helped me...
- One big life lesson I learned while growing up is...
- Why I care so much about personal development and lifelong learning is...

- One or two failures in my life and the lessons I learned from them

My Values

My own values are quite personal to me, as yours are to you. Yet with the coarsening of our discourse in politics, social media, and mainstream media, experts say leaders sharing their values with their teams has become critically important for many reasons.

Examples of My Values:

- Being generous in all aspects of life
- Giving without expectations
- Loyalty and compassion
- Always moving forward…never standing still
- Personal growth
- Humility
- Risk taking and innovation

My Beliefs

Beliefs are ideas a person holds as being true. Perceptions are beliefs about how the world seems to be, based on the evidence one has— "earth is flat or round." Opinions are beliefs about how one should interpret reality. Predictions are beliefs about how one thinks things will end up in the future based on what one knows now. Metas are one's beliefs about beliefs, e.g., "Everyone has the right to have their own beliefs."

Examples of My Beliefs:

- The road to excellence is endless
- Patients deserve a "Wow" experience
- Your success is not what you do, it is how you do it
- Continuing education throughout life is critical for lasting success

- You must spend money to make money

My Definition of Excellence

One definition for personal excellence is a continuous process in being consistent in good character, attitude, quality, and standards. In the dental industry, the pursuit of excellence is rooted in continuous improvement and patient-centered care. The three domains of excellence for dental practices are clinical competency, patient satisfaction, and profitability. Excellence in dental practice management can be categorized as systems, procedures, and communication. Evidence-based dentistry is based on three domains: the best scientific evidence, the patient's individual needs and preferences, and the dentist's clinical skill and judgment.

For this team meeting, you will likely define excellence in the domains of systems, procedures, communication, team member interaction and collaboration, and patient satisfaction. Some dentists even share the finances of the practice, especially when providing profit-sharing. Pursuing consistency across all locations and maintaining a company culture of excellence is rewarding yet seemingly never-ending. The importance of clarifying this for your team members is that without a goal or target clearly defined, there is no measure of success.

Examples:

- Daily preparation for each patient's care; patient record reviews
- Treatment conversation results
- Incidents of post-treatment issues is less than X%
- Commitment to doing what is best for the patient
- Patient experience is consistently one of high quality that delights and exceeds our patient's expectations—results of surveys, reviews
- We don't tolerate mediocrity, are not satisfied with average, and go the extra mile in all endeavors
- Number of patient referrals each month

"They actually saw me! They cared so much about me."
—Jason Alejos

"I didn't leave my house for over 2 years. I didn't socialize or anything. I had lost all my confidence!

I did lots of research for a long time. I chose Dr. Sean and his team because of the way they treated me and how they were genuinely concerned about me as a person. Everything about them was top notch, excellent. My procedure was seamless and pain free. They restored my confidence and I felt like the "real me" for the first time in years!"

Our Definition of Success

Defining success is like excellence, yet in this context, success is primarily defined as the behaviors team members will practice, and outcomes they will achieve through collaboration, support, and interaction amongst themselves, and for the patients. The definition of success is a cornerstone to building your company culture. Implementing behavior standards is the proven method to ensure lasting success (see *People* section).

Examples:

- Team members always feel respected, included, and safe at work
- Team members do not triangulate or gossip—team member concerned about a coworker, discusses their concern with them first, always "assuming the best"
- Difficult conversations among peers are done with the spirit of "I care enough to tell you" (reframing conflict avoidance)
- Team members respect the importance of budgets and financials by minimizing waste and maintaining productivity
- Team members provide exceptional service recovery with dissatisfied patients, without defensiveness or blame

My Expectations of Myself and Our Team Members

> One of the most common causes of strife in relationships is unclear or unmet expectations. This is especially true at work.

Sharing the expectations, you have of yourself humanizes you as the owner, and is received by your team members as vulnerability and openness on your part. Clarifying expectations of your team members creates 'rules to live by' and boundaries.

After this meeting, your top performers and informal group leaders are far more likely to speak up with a coworker who is not abiding by the expectations. Again, implementing behavior standards helps with expectations.

Examples:

- Take responsibility for your choices, actions, results, and impact on others
- Strive to learn and improve…do not settle and become complacent
- "Work smart and work hard" and hustle in the pursuit of excellence
- Be humble, open to feedback and coaching with gratitude
- Always focus on moving forward and making things better (give examples)
- Speak up: When you see something say something…Be constructive, respectful, and thoughtful
- Choose to be positive at work…Leave drama at home
- Always Assume the Best of One Another, Manage Up and No Triangulation

In Support of You and Your Teams

Publicly sharing what you will do specifically to support each team member goes a long way to squelch any rumblings of negativity among team members. It clarifies expectations and boundaries, so everyone is aware of this support. Again, this models your humility and genuine concern as their leader and builds trust with them.

Examples:

I will…

- Consistently and frequently ask questions to better understand your work experience
- Solicit your input and suggestions more often and provide timely feedback
- Meet quarterly with the team to discuss what is working well and what is not
- Start sharing more of the reasoning behind why we can or can't do something
- Support you by providing training opportunities whenever possible
- Meet with each of you one-on-one, quarterly, to discuss your progress and professional development

Presentation Wrap Up

After you finish your presentation, one of the most powerful, effective, and efficient ways to wrap this meeting up is to ask your team members to pair up in small groups of two or three people, and simply share with one another what they heard you just share; what stood out to them; what was most important; and what they appreciate the most. Give them three to five minutes for this discussion.

Then bring them back together and either ask for people to share a thought from their group discussions or invite anyone to ask clarifying questions. Focusing on clarifying questions is best, rather than just asking for questions. You want this portion of your meeting to end on a positive note.

While this may seem like a lot of work to prepare, or you may be questioning the value of doing this, I have received great value from these meetings, with multiple benefits. You will likely see shifts in attitude, demeanor, energy, communication, and interaction among your team members. You will see who is "on board" and who may have missed the message or is still not "on board." And best of all, your leaders, managers, supervisors, informal group leaders, and top performers will be grateful for you and your message, especially clarifying expectations and the definitions of excellence and success.

Chapter 16
REFLECTION: Employee Engagement: The Key to Success

1. What are my values and beliefs, personally and professionally?

2. What are my definitions of excellence? For...

    - Evidence-based dentistry
    - Practice management—systems, procedures, communication
    - Patient Satisfaction and Experience
    - Clinical Outcomes
    - Business and Financial Results

3. What are three expectations of myself that will help me achieve the most important goals, personally, and for the business?

Chapter 16
ACTION:
Employee Engagement: The Key to Success

1. Select a group of team members and invite them to provide you with their own definitions of excellence and success in whichever categories or domains you wish.

2. Meet with your practice manager and supervisors and invite them to share their definitions of excellence and success; expectations of team members; and the best ways you can support your team members.

3. Identify a quality improvement task force (short-term project) and ask them to analyze the biggest opportunities to improve in pursuit of excellence in the domains of procedures, systems, communication, and patient satisfaction.

The following tools are available here:
www.TheresNoStandingStill.com

Reality Check: The Positives & Challenges of Dentistry & What to Do About It

Your Team Culture Blueprint

CHAPTER 17

Strengthening Your Leadership and Executive Teams

"Failing organizations are usually over-managed and under-led."
–Warren Bennis

Straight out of dental school I was a one-man show for a long time. I paid the price in many ways, professionally and personally. After my divorce, I realized I was alone again. The difference was that I had the wisdom this time; to know how to achieve my personal and professional goals, I can't do all this alone. It takes people around me to be successful and to achieve the goals I have for my dental practices, 4M Institute, and my life outside of work. New relationships have been helpful in all aspects of my life. The growth of our 4M Institute with Julieanne O'Connor, being coached by Steve Sperry, experiencing the Lotus Leadership Event, and writing this book with my publishing partner, all came from new relationships.

The two teams which have enabled me to grow my business into multiple practices and to create 4M Institute are my Executive Team and our Leadership Team. Our Leadership Team oversees daily operations of our multiple dental practices. We now have a General Manager who is responsible for all aspects of operations across all locations. Each location has an office manager/practice manager who reports to the General Manager. Hiring a General Manager is one of the best decisions I've made because it has enabled me to focus on the bigger picture of my business and 4M Institute. Once I started investing in leaders to grow my business, and I let go of my tendency for micromanaging and control, I became a true business owner/ entrepreneur, evolving from a highly paid practitioner.

Evolution isn't easy.

> Letting go of the day-to-day reins of the operation, putting trust in my team leaders and team members is not easy. It took time, especially for the first several years of my practice. In fact, my experience tells me you will be far more successful, far more quickly, when you hire a trusted business coach and learn from peers who are successfully further along the journey.

For far too many years, I did all the inventorying and ordering myself. My rationale was based mostly on "the significant amount of money tied up in inventory" and "how many different items there were to track."

One day, reflecting upon what I had heard so many times from various advisors, coaches, and my own team leaders, I finally surrendered. I remember realizing I would never be able to grow my business to the size and scale I envisioned, without letting go, trusting others, and trusting the process. I immediately started training someone to take over inventory management and ordering of supplies. This person took pride in her work, was conscientious, and she became proficient quickly. She did it as well as I did, and even better in some ways.

Dentists who participate in our advanced dentistry courses at 4M Institute often have similar stories wishing they had "let go and trusted others" many years earlier. The key to change and growth is to be humble and open to the advice, counsel, and input of others.

My Executive Team includes my General Manager, a business/leadership coach, the Director of 4M Institute, a CPA, and an attorney. Additional professional advisors include a business mentor, a mentor dentist, a few peer dentists, a financial advisor, and an investments advisor. Periodically, I may have a business consultant working on a specific business challenge or project, as well.

This chapter shares wisdom from my business coach, Steve Sperry, and my publishing partner, who is a 25-year change management consultant and former Walt Disney World leader and trainer.

The Value of an Hour

Before we explore your leadership and management skills, it is important to understand what an hour of your life is worth. Socrates is credited for espousing, "An unexamined life is not worth living," resulting in humans being deprived of the meaning and purpose of existence. Failing to know the value of an hour of your life, similarly, deprives you of the ability to make decisions and understand the true value of your time and energy–both precious and limited for all of us.

Attorneys bill their clients by the hour. Attorney fees range from $150/hour to $1200/hour. Yes, $1200. What specifically does a $1200/hour attorney do, or what value are they bringing their clients that is worthy of this fee?

The dividend of your work with patients lasts a lifetime. The dividend of your coaching a team member lasts their entire career, perhaps a lifetime. What's the dividend to you and your family, from working 50-60 hours a week, 50 weeks out of the year?

Each year, you work 2500 to 3000 hours. Take a moment and tally your total income from the work you do every day. You have other income as well from investments, real estate, etc. Yet for now, we are looking at your total income earned from work, after taxes.

For example, after taxes, a dentist may earn $150,000 per year. Another may earn $400,000.

Therefore,

$150,000 divided by 2500 hours equals $60/hour
$150,000 divided by 3000 hours equals $50/hour

$400,000 divided by 2500 hours equals $160/hour
$400,000 divided by 3000 hours equals $133/hour

Knowing this one data point informs your decisions, perhaps in a way you have not considered. Instead of you conducting the inventory of supplies each week, which takes 2 hours, imagine training one of your team members to do it instead.

Supply Inventory:

- At $60/hour, when you complete the 2-hour inventory, it costs your practice $120.
- At $22/hour, when your team member completes it, it costs your practice $44.
- This one change saves your practice $76/week, or $3,952/year.

Your Opportunity

When any task you complete can be completed, as well or better, by someone else on your team, you have a huge opportunity with multiple payoffs.

- You save your practice money (or free you up to do more valuable work)
- Your team member learns a new task, possibly increasing their job satisfaction
- You may retain this team member longer
- You may get the work done better, faster or more consistently
- You remove an energy drain from your work life–you did not go to Dental school so you could do supply inventory 52 weeks a year
- You may get home two hours earlier one day per week–game night, date night, and see your kid's school play?

Best of all, you may begin to reclaim your own life, your own time, save energy, and enjoy your work life more.

Game Changer

Let's say you have ten hours of work each week, conservatively, which you are doing, that could be delegated to a team member or leader. This work would be done for less, even way less, than your $60/hour. Then, DELEGATE. Sure, you may need to train them first, yet what a small price to invest, to free yourself from the task, for the rest of your life!

The transformational ripple effect potential in your business is when you take this same logic and calculation to assess what your practice manager, associate dentists, and team leads are doing every week, which could be delegated to a team member for less expense and with the ROI benefits mentioned above. Various studies have shown that owners, senior leaders, and mid-level leaders of companies spend 10-40 hours per month doing the work that someone else could/should be doing. This is an age-old epidemic in business today.

> Anything you need to get done that can be done for less, you get to delegate or outsource.

It Takes a Team

Finding the right people does not mean finding the "absolute best people," it means finding right-fit people. This is true from your frontline staff to your Executive Team. What makes someone right for your team? Just like finding the right mix of players on a sports team, the right players must perform well together. They must be equally fit, able to communicate effectively, and in alignment with your mission, vision, and goals. Trust, loyalty, maturity, and commitment are also big factors in creating a successful team.

The best teams are made up of team members who respect one another and honor their differences and unique gifts. Having the balance of knowing one's own "zone of genius" and the humility "to know I don't know what I don't know," serves every team member and contributes to a team culture of humility, and listening to "understand first, then to be understood."

Depending on where you are in your journey, your executive team might have a mix of in-house and outsourced members. Your leadership team will likely be fully in-house leaders. A typical starting point for building your in-house leadership team is the office manager/practice manager. From there, you might add team leads for hygiene, back-office assistants, and front-office administrators. A few logical team members to outsource are the marketing person, lab tech, Coach/Trainer, CPA (financial advisor), and legal counsel.

To establish your team, there are expert resources available to offer you guidance. For example, Burkheart, Patterson, and Shein have some talented people willing to help you find the best team members for you. Even manufacturer reps have talent and know talented people. There are also many new groups like the D.E.O. (Jake Puhl, CEO) that exclusively works with dentists to find the best executive team and resources to grow your practice.

Great leaders attract great executive teams and retain members of their leadership team. When was the last time you invested in your own leadership skills?

"Leadership is the process of social influence in which one person can enlist the aid and support of others in the accomplishment of a common task."

Presidential biographer and leadership expert James MacGregor Burns coined the phrase "transformational leadership" defining it as a process in which "leaders and followers help each other to advance to a higher level of morale and motivation."

Burns described two different leadership concepts: transformational leadership and transactional leadership. According to Burns, the transforming approach creates a significant change in the life of people and organizations. Transformational leaders focus on followers, motivating them to high levels of performance, and in the process, help followers develop their own leadership potential.

Transformational leaders inspire followers to change expectations, perceptions, and motivations to work toward common goals through the strength of their vision and personality.

> Transformational leaders engage and equip team members to take greater ownership of their roles and responsibilities, which gives them greater purpose and meaning to their work, while also enabling leaders to focus on achieving their vision and goals.

Warren Bennis, a renowned leadership expert said, “Failing organizations are usually over-managed and under-led.” If we are transactional in our business, it’s difficult to be relational, connecting, and empathizing with our team and patients. My willingness to relinquish supply inventory and ordering enabled me to reclaim the time lost from a transactional focus which robs me of the opportunity to focus and achieve my most important high-value activities. When you find yourself thinking “I am so busy,” or, “Time flew today, yet what did I really accomplish today?” consider asking yourself these questions:

- Am I busy doing my best, most important, highest-value activities, or am I spending way too much time doing tactical, transactional activities (no matter the reason or excuse)?
- Who could be doing this instead of me? (Remember “the value of an hour of your time”)
- What would it take to transition this work to them?
- What are the “real reasons” I won’t let go and let someone else take over this activity? (Hint: fear(s), limiting belief, lack of experience, perfectionism, control)
- What is this costing me/us? (Hint: burnout, resentment, exhaustion, depression, high turnover, team losing trust in me, only one location, no business growth, financial loss)

Identifying what drives your decisions and choices is key to your growth and change.

Asking "Who and What" questions is productive. Now is not the time to worry about "How" to fix this–the "how" will come from reading, asking your coach and even your peers. Asking "How" questions, at this point, creates far too many opportunities to focus, even obsess, on the wrong things, often leading to spinning your wheels, overwhelm, avoidance, or "shut down."

Are You a Manager or a Leader?

Behind every system is a team member. Finding the right team members is crucial to our success. Managing is the easy part. Leading your people and building something special with your team and your practice is much harder, especially for dentists. Over the years I've learned to develop teams, not just manage processes and systems 24/7. Make no mistake, everyone is doing their jobs well, accountability and productivity are critical to our success. Yet hiring, inspiring, and keeping that superstar team is the foundation of team success in the short-term and especially in the long-term. Shifting from Manager to Leader, frankly, is one of the "secrets to my success." In fact, I only began adding new locations and truly growing my company after I made this profound paradigm shift.

We can hire managers that have the knowledge to manage. What we need are leaders who are inspired by a worthy cause to change lives and give patients their smiles back. This begins with you becoming a true leader.

"One of the true measures of effective leadership:
Do your team and your operations function
as well or better in your absence?"

Your goal is to have teams and operations that run better, even far better, in your absence. Our Las Vegas practice has achieved this. Our success comes when I lead, coach, and support them, especially in developing our associate dentists. This all started with letting go of my need to control and micromanage, hiring great people, trusting them, letting them take ownership of their work and their results, getting out of their way, and simply supporting them and coaching them along the way.

In a moment you will see two lists of questions and statements. One list is what you may be asking or saying when you are in Transactional Manager Mode. The other list is what you may be asking or saying when you are in Transformational Leader Mode.

Give yourself the opportunity to explore how much of each day you spend in Transactional Manager mode or Transformational Leader mode. You may be surprised. The *Management versus Leadership Self-Assessment* is available on the resource website.

Questions or Statements in "Transactional Manager Mode"

- If I want it done right, I have to/must do it myself.
- I must see more patients every day.
- My people just don't care as much as I do about the patients and doing great work.
- I just can't find good people who are willing to work hard and do quality work.
- Some of my people need to grow up. I feel like I'm babysitting, not managing.
- If they don't do the work, they've got to go. Everyone can be replaced.
- How many appointment slots went unfilled today, and whose fault is it?
- Our practice isn't growing because I don't have enough good people.

Questions or Statements in "Transformational Leader Mode"

- Have I created a workplace that communicates clear expectations, provides the tools my people need to do their best work and builds trust and safety, so co-workers speak freely?
- What can I do differently to inspire and engage more of my team members to work hard and hustle to benefit our patients? Am I a great role model?
- Am I paying a competitive wage that enables us to attract the best people?
- Based on our numbers and metrics, what is working well? What do my team members think we can do to improve?
- What do I need to do to address the non-performers and "Negative Nancy's" on our team?
- Everyone's performance and results reflect how effectively I lead, train, and develop them.
- Have I built a workplace culture of high performance through accountability and collaboration?
- Do I consistently have a current pulse of whether our patients are truly satisfied, and whether we are delivering exceptional service and patient experiences?

Your opportunity now is to simply identify and address how much time you are spending, managing versus leading. Assess the same for each of your leaders.

To inspire you with practical real-world opportunities for improvement, consider the ROI you will achieve by addressing this leadership opportunity, especially regarding:

- Patient experience, satisfaction, and outcomes
- Client retention and referrals
- Employee turnover and retention
- Growth of your people and your practice

- Financial performance and business outcomes
- Your own satisfaction at work, with less stress and burnout

Million-Dollar Questions

- What is an hour of my time worth?
- How much time do I spend managing versus leading?
- How much time, energy, and money do I invest in becoming a better leader?
- Does my practice manager make time to lead, or just spend all day managing?
- Do I hire leaders, or do I hire technicians and managers and just call them leaders?
- Do I know what drives and inspires each of my team members to do great work, focus on our patients, and pursue excellence in all ways?
- Am I willing to admit to myself my shortcomings as a leader, and do what it takes to become a better leader?

Chapter 17
REFLECTION: Strengthening Your Leadership and Executive Teams

1. In my own practice, if I were a team member, would I follow me as the owner/leader?

2. Do I run my business and lead in such a way that others would enthusiastically want to join my executive team?

3. Do I believe in and respect the principle that "relationships at work matter?"

4. Do I believe and respect that the work culture of my practice and the healthiness/effectiveness of my team members are the results of my own ability to manage and lead?

5. Do I have a compelling vision for our practice that is far more than just clinical excellence and patient outcomes?

6. If someone privately asked each of my team members what our compelling vision is, would everyone state the same vision?

7. If I could change any one thing about my own leadership skills, what would I change?

8. What am I willing to do to make things the way I want them to be?

9. Who is a transformational leader from whom I can learn (ask for mentoring)?

10. What happens, good and bad, if I do nothing to improve my leadership skills?

11. Do my team and our operations function as well or better in my absence? How am I holding my team back from taking full ownership when I am absent?

Chapter 17
ACTION:
Strengthening Your Leadership and Executive Teams

1. What specific steps can you take to improve your leadership skills?
   You may wish to attend Lotus Leadership Event https://inventivedentalsolutions.com/ I've attended a few times and I learn something about myself, my leadership, and what I can do better as a leader, every time I attend.

2. What is your compelling vision for your practice?
   (More than just your tagline or jingle–your why, your purpose, your goals)

3. When you hire a business/leadership coach, your top three improvement areas are:

4. What leadership practices could you do every day, even just fifteen minutes per day, to improve yourself, your team, your practice, or your patient experience?

5. Bring together a few of your trusted frontline leaders from various departments and have a frank conversation with them about what you can do differently to enable them to take full ownership of the practice, especially when you are absent. What training or information or experience do they need? Are you micromanaging? What do you need to stop doing yourself, and let them handle it? (Tip: Prior to these conversations you can invite everyone to complete the Stop, Start, Continue Exercise so you have some feedback prior to your meeting.)

The following tools are available here:
www.TheresNoStandingStill.com

Stop, Start, Continue Feedback Exercise

Management versus Leadership Self-Assessment

CHAPTER 18

Work Less. Earn More. Change Lives.™

"It's hard to be a lighthouse for others if you can't keep your own lights on."
—Erin Loman Jeck

I wrote this book to save you ten years of strife, struggle, stress, overwhelm, burnout and *trial by fire*. I am forever grateful for what I learned in dental school, the mentors who shaped my thinking and guided me along the way, and the clinical skills I gained. However, there is so much more to the reality of what it takes to succeed as a dentist, an entrepreneur, and a good human being.

William G. Dickerson, DDS, FAACD, LVIM, FIAPA, LVIF, mentored me in dentistry and entrepreneurship. Just as his words of wisdom taught me what is possible to truly succeed, I hope you have found this book to be informative, inspiring, equipping, engaging, and empowering. No matter how long it has been since you graduated from dental school, may you keep an open mind to what is possible for you. May you challenge your own thinking, stoke your curiosity, and amass the confidence to take risks and invest in yourself and your future. Your patients are waiting for you. You deserve to have the life of your dreams without spending 80 hours a week at the office.

Dr. Dickerson was an extremely successful dentist in Las Vegas, who built such a successful practice he was able to sell it and created the Las Vegas Institute for Advanced Dental Studies (LVI Global). His Institute was successful because he followed his dream and passion and took a risk. The risk paid off when he sold LVI Global to a private equity firm as well. He taught cosmetic dentistry and wrote the book, *Unleashing the Power of Dentistry: An Introduction to Neuromuscular Dentistry.* He showed me the importance of being proud of what we do as dentists. He taught me how to have more respect for what we do and how to get paid what we deserve, while providing exceptional quality care and patient outcomes.

Sadly, he is right when he says most dentists don't respect themselves nor what they do as a profession, and too often feel guilty about charging higher fees. I remember thinking, "If he can build a successful practice, sell it, and start an institute for the advancement of our profession, then why can't I?" How about you? Now that you have read this book, imagine what is possible for you, your people, your patients, and your practice.

Throughout this book you have learned what is working well for successful dental practices and exactly what you can do to achieve excellence and build the life you want and deserve, while transforming lives every day. This book wouldn't be complete however, if I didn't share insights from my years of building multiple profitable practices. Profit is not the only purpose for what we do day-in and day-out. Profit is an engine that fuels our continued success. Profit reflects our ability to provide exceptional value and quality outcomes, at a fair price, while also managing our business and leading our people in ways that enable us to build a company that matters. A company that exists as much for the family of team members within it as it does for the patients it serves.

Profits With a Purpose

Whether you want to keep your solo-practice healthy and growing, or you want to build your own large DSO, having a compelling purpose beyond *making money* is what will help you weather the storms of tough times, and find meaning in what you are doing for yourself, your people, and your patients. The following *Profit Drivers* are levers to push as you grow your practice or multiple practices. Twice a year, when you are working on your business not in your business, tending to your business plan and strategic plan, invest time to take a hard look at your own Profit Drivers.

It's Not a New Patient Problem

Profitability and continued success in the growth of your practice(s) is based far more on case acceptance, optimizing hygiene appointments, minimizing cancellations, providing IV sedation and multiple services, boosting employee engagement and retention, and providing a great guest experience, than whether you are getting more new patients. Profits lie within the patients you already serve and the optimization of your practice.

De novo versus Acquisition

If I had a choice, I would add de novo practices (new start-ups) because when you are building new construction you have ultimate control of all facets of the practice—technology, size, number of operatories, equipment, team members, construction, and design. However, it takes time, usually 2+ years, to achieve EBITDA, Earnings Before Interest, Taxes, Depreciation, and Amortization. It also requires upfront capital investment, oftentimes at least $1.5M or more.

Whereas, when acquiring an existing practice, it is already generating revenue with cashflow, and hopefully profits. However, oftentimes you must terminate many team members due to their poor habits or performance, invest significant time and money in training of all staff, replace technology and equipment, deal with aging facilities, and possibly associate dentists who are not up to par for your expectations.

Case Acceptance

Successful Treatment Conversations (case acceptance) start with your confidence and level of certainty that you know, without a doubt, you can help your patients. Offering multiple services under one roof, practicing the Magic 5, and simplifying things for patients (not too many options), are critical to your success. Always remember, a confused patient never invests.

Bigger Cases

Working Less comes when you are doing large cases, more complex procedures, or taking care of multiple services at once. As I've said several times, providing IV Sedation is the linchpin to expanding your service capabilities. The math is simple…2 or 3 $50,000 Teeth-in-One-Day procedures or 20+ cosmetic dentistry patients?

Drop Dental Insurances

When you accept dental insurances, you become forced to do many more procedures to earn a living, not to mention the cost of tracking everything, and the headaches for you and your billing staff. To drop dental insurances is not a choice to be made quickly, without serious consideration. Providing multiple services and having the confidence to charge what you deserve are cornerstones to your ability to drop insurances.

Know Your Numbers

There are several numbers you must learn to track to be a successful entrepreneur dentist. Knowing your numbers, managing your business based on real numbers in a timely manner, and making informed decisions definitively, are business skills present in all extremely successful practices. If this is not your strong suit, then consult your CPA, hire a business coach, or hire a CFO-type team member. The critically important numbers are:

Revenue production per hour	Cash flow
Average charge per treatment	Expense ratios
Overhead costs	Operating margin
Patient receivables	Employee productivity and efficiency

Pre-procedure Collections

Collecting payments from patients prior to procedures being performed is critical to maintain healthy positive cash flow. While cash flow is not directly *profit,* it is the lifeblood of your practice, nonetheless. Pre-collection decreases cancellations and reduces patients' anxiety (everyone hates paying when they walk in). Therefore, if it is pre-paid patients don't have to think about payments every time they go to the dentist.

Mortal Marketing Mistake

Too often I hear dentists say things like, "I stopped paying for those ads, they weren't working." Cutting back on marketing is not the answer, maximizing marketing conversion is. Always know what the cost of acquisition of a new patient is for your practice. Also figure out what conversion rates are required in order for your marketing efforts to be self-liquidating, e.g., Facebook ads which generate $2.80 for every $1.00 spent on FB ads.

Recording Calls

Like maximizing marketing conversion, investing time, energy and money into listening to your team members' patient phone calls pays multiple dividends. As Steve Sperry explained in the chapter,

Connecting and Converting Patients by Phone, you could be missing out on $50,000 procedures because of what only one team member is saying, or not saying, on the phone.

Missing Page in Your Business Plan

I learned many years ago, the single page missing from most business plans is the last page. It turns out, billionaires, private equity, and angel investors, are looking for this page every time they consider investing or acquiring a business. The page includes names of those who will acquire your company in 10 years from now. Including this page shows them you have a vision beyond owning a solo-practice and have the courage to dream and aspire to great growth. For you, this page can inform you the way you make financial decisions as you move forward. For instance, are you building your company to maximize profits every year, or maximize growth to be acquired in the future?

Purposeful Profits

Leading and managing profitable dental practices has given me a family of more than 100 team members, and nine practices by the end of this year. Starting with Las Vegas, we have added Anaheim Hills, Long Beach, Newport Beach, Murrieta, Valencia, Palm Desert, Riverside, and San Diego. We are now performing several thousand All-on-4 procedures, and hundreds of restorative and cosmetic procedures each year.

Most important to me are the 100+ team members, because without them we have no patients. I consider these great people my extended family. I am so proud and grateful to hear when one of my team members can buy their first car, or their first home, are able to get a much-needed surgery or treatment, finish their degree, start college, go on vacation for the first time in years, or support their own parents in transition. It has been a thrill over the years to see team members start in entry-level positions who are now in critical roles at levels of our organization.

My hope for you is that you will find meaning and purpose in building a company and a team who transform the lives of your patients. I hope you now see the potential in yourself, your people, your patients, and your practice! And most of all, always remember…

There's no standing still!

Chapter 18
REFLECTION:
Work Less. Earn More. Change Lives.™

1. Do I know my numbers and am I tracking them frequently enough to make meaningful timely decisions for the growth of my business?

2. Which business numbers or performance metrics do I get to spend more time on to understand them and utilize them better in my decision making?

3. What does "profitable" mean to me right now, and in the future, as I grow my practice(s)?

4. What is my potential as I look back on all that I have learned from this book?

5. Which Profit Drivers would make the greatest impact on profitability over the next few months and beyond?

6. What is the purpose that drives me in building this practice(s)?

Chapter 18
ACTION:
Work Less. Earn More. Change Lives.™

1. What specific steps can you take to improve your performance metric tracking?

2. What is your compelling vision for your practice?

3. What specific steps can you take to improve profitability?

4. On the last page of your business plan, "Who Acquires Us," who will acquire your business 10 years from now? Or if acquisition is not the goal, what is the definition of a "profitable practice" based on your priorities and values?

The following tools are available here:
www.TheresNoStandingStill.com

Costly Mistakes to Avoid in Growing Your Dental Practice Checklist

Best Practices in Growing from One Practice to Multiple Locations

Most Important Success Factors in Growing a Profitable Dental Practice

The 10 Performance Metrics Every Successful Dentist Entrepreneur Tracks

7 Best Practices to Pre-Collect Funds from Patients Prior to Procedures

In Memoriam

Dr. Ben Javid

A heart of gold, a smile of pure joy, a kindness extended to all he knew, with masterful skill and passion for changing lives. This was Dr. Ben Javid.

Dr. Ben Javid, prosthodontist, lead educator at 4M Institute, mentor, father, peer, and dear friend, we are deeply grateful for the difference you made in all our lives.

Rarely have I met a person who lights up a room, shares joy and laughter, and shares their knowledge and experience as generously as Dr. Javid. From the first day we met at a local coffee shop, Dr. Javid was a fan of our vision for the 4M Institute and 4M Dental Implant Center. I discovered quickly how smart and capable he was, and he knew as much as I did about full-arch restorations and even more about restorative dentistry.

He was our first dentist in our Long Beach practice, and his contributions still shine through to this day. He helped design the 4M Institute and was an integral faculty member. He was a natural-born teacher and mentor, who so passionately and humbly shared his wisdom and experience with his peers and our 4M Institute graduates.

Whenever I had a challenging case Dr. Javid was always the first person I called. Our staff and associates fondly say, "Dr. Javid would have known what to do." He changed the smiles and lives of almost 3000 patients. As a teacher and mentor, his legacy lives on within so many staff and dentists. As a kind and generous friend and peer, his legacy of caring deeply for one another and encouraging others to have their best lives is in all of us who were blessed to have known him.

You will never be forgotten and may your memory be forever held in our hearts.

988 Suicide and Crisis Lifeline

If you or someone you know, has a mental illness, is struggling emotionally, or has concerns about their mental health, call or text 988, to connect with a trained crisis counselor.
Or use **Lifeline Chat** on the web (English only) via https://988lifeline.org/chat/

If you or someone you know, has a mental illness, is struggling emotionally, or has concerns about their mental health, call or text 988, to connect with a trained crisis counselor. Or use Lifeline Chat on the web (English only) via https://988lifeline.org/chat/

The Lifeline provides 24-hour, confidential support to anyone in suicidal crisis or emotional distress.

Acknowledgments

To my mother and father, thank you for the gift of life you have given me. Everything I have is because of your hard work, dedication, and love. I am forever grateful for both of you.

To my 3 beautiful daughters, Lily, Tara, and Ayla. You are my life, my heartbeat, and my inspiration to be a better person every day. To their mom Samira, thank you for your never-ending love and support of our daughters and me, you are amazing.

To my brothers, Hamid, Jalal, and Masoud. Thank you for your constant support and always pushing me to succeed.

To our patients, I cherish each one of you and I am thankful for the trust you have put in our hands to help you live your best life with a healthy and beautiful smile!

To my amazing team, Dr. Derik, Traci, Shadi, Kayla, Melissa, Kim, Luis, and the rest of our team members who pursue excellence for our patients every day. Thank you for your loyalty. You all have a special place in my life.

To my professors, teachers, mentors and coaches, Julieanne O'Connor, Steve Sperry, Steven Rowell, Sensei Greg, you all have inspired me in different ways.

To my special friends, Bijan, Saman, Afshins, Steve and Bruce, I am forever grateful for your friendship. To Michelle Bartfay, thank you for being an integral part of my life and making a profound difference. Your presence filled my journey with joy and meaning.

To our 4M Institute faculty and students, Dr. Athena Goodarzi, Dr. T. Emadi, Dr. Jordan Colby, Dr. Ramin Moradi, Dr. Samira Houshiar and many more, your courageous pursuit of learning new skills, and delivering excellence in every way has given me great purpose and meaning in my life. You all are the reason we built 4M Institute, so we may continue changing the world one smile at a time.

About the Author

Dr. Sean is the founder of 4M Institute and is known for his expertise in dental implant solutions. He operates multiple dental practices and established the 4M Institute to provide comprehensive training for dentists in various areas, such as clinical and lab training, marketing, sales, and leadership.

Dr. Sean recognizes the importance of post-graduate training and has created a state-of-the-art facility with advanced technology and top-of-the-line equipment to ensure students have access to cutting-edge tools. He has extensive hands-on training experience and understands how it can elevate a dental practice to the next level.

One of Dr. Sean's strengths is his ability to identify potential patients in a rapidly growing market. He shares this knowledge with dentists in his courses, helping them develop the skills necessary to handle cases ranging from $20,000 to $50,000. Additionally, Dr. Sean travels around the world to deliver lectures.

The World Headquarters of 4M Institute serves as the institute itself and one of Dr. Sean's leading dental implant practices, the 4M Dental Implant Center.

Dr. Sean Mohtashami
Founder, 4M Institute &
4M Dental Implant Center

Contributing Author

Steven Rowell

Change Management Consultant,
Mastermind Producer,
Speaker & Philanthropist

Steven is the founder of Accelerated Ventures and co-founder of Accelerator Forum, helping successful business consultants and coaches earn more by licensing their best programs to corporations, growing with strategic partnerships, and hosting business growth forums. His corporate consulting includes helping companies focused on high performance and profitability by building a service excellence culture with great entrepreneurial leaders at every level.

He has provided consulting and training to 24 Fortune 500 companies such as UPS, Walmart, Compass, Shell, Pfizer, and Huntsman. He also licensed his patient satisfaction improvement system to 1100 hospitals nationwide. He credits much of his success to the seven years he spent opening new resorts for Walt Disney World and facilitating a new hire orientation called *Traditions* at Disney University.

Steven has hosted many accelerated business growth forums (masterminds) for business owners from fifteen industries. Forum members have generated more than $124 million in new revenue using only three or four of his business growth strategies.

He is the author of multiple books, including *Success from the Inside Out; Jumpstart Your Creativity;* and *How to Connect with Anyone, Anywhere at Any Time (2023),* with 210,000 books distributed globally.

He has shared stages with Sir Richard Branson, Les Brown, Jack Canfield, Kim Walsh Phillips, Brendon Burchard, Ryan Levesque, Rich Schefren, Stu Mclaren, Harvey Mackay, Tom Peters, Brian Scudamore, Tim Ferris, Michael Eisner, Brian Tracy, and Coach Lou Holtz.

Steven performed improv with Wayne Brady in Las Vegas, and he occasionally can be heard impersonating Mickey Mouse, Goofy, and Eeyore. He and his wife, an acclaimed filmmaker, producer, and podcaster, have one son in college, and one foster daughter in Cape Town, South Africa.

Contributing Author

Julieanne O'Connor

International Speaker &
INFLUENCE COACH
for High-Achieving Dentists & CEOs,
Bestselling Author, TEDx Speaker,
Certified Corporate
Trainer, Strategic Intervention Coach
& Strategist, Marketing & Leadership Expert

Julieanne O'Connor helps high-achieving CEOs and Dentists to leverage their influence because they are often overworked and overwhelmed. O'Connor provides dentists and their teams with powerful strategies for goals and implementation, effective leadership, team building, branding, PR and social media, as well as "quality of life" and "burnout prevention". O'Connor offers private coaching to select high-achievers and lectures internationally for specialists, high-profile companies, training institutes, study clubs, DSOs, and select other practices.

O'Connor is a bestselling author on the faculty of 4M Institute and ADI (American Dental Institute), and is the CEO of Animal Impulse, Ltd. (InfluentialDentists.com), Director of ZLinked Marketing & Advertising, and the Co-founder of the Nano Podcast Alliance for Dentists. O'Connor is an award-winning author and actor who has been named "Best New Author" by Amazon and is a star of the award-winning Superbowl commercial *Doritos Pug Attack*.

O'Connor has been named "Speaker of the Year" and has been featured on Adweek, Adage, WSJ, CNN, USA Today, to name a few. She has worked with and/or helped launch some of the most well-known brands in America. O'Connor is the producer of dental leadership programs and retreats. She can be heard on countless dental podcasts and more, has been published in numerous articles, and can be seen on stages worldwide. Having started from humble beginnings where she grew up on contaminated property initially with no plumbing, O'Connor is committed to the ongoing study of "the human condition". O'Connor is a wife, mother, foster mom, adoptive mom, and the founder of the SIO Dream Fund.

Training Topics & Keynotes

Influence (Secrets of Influential Dentists), Branding, Marketing & Social Media for Dentists, Elite Team Training & Emotional Intelligence, Leadership, How to Interact with Patients (Listening/Closing), Burnout Prevention for Dentists & their Teams, Strategy & Execution, Goal Setting & Implementation, Quality of Life (Growth/Giving), Powerful Strategies for Growth, Team Training for High Ticket Cases, Accountability and Follow-Through, Motivation for Growth

CONTACT
Website: InfluentialDentists.com
Phone: 818-749-5598
Email: InfluentialDentists@gmail.com
Insta/Twitter: @spellingit
Facebook/Pinterest: @spellingitout
LinkedIn: https://www.linkedin.com/in/julieanneoconnor/

Contributing Author

Steve Sperry

Owner, Inventive Dental Solutions
Founder, LOTUS Leadership Program
for Dental Professionals
Faculty Member, 4M Institute

Steve's passion is to train dentists to become leaders who own a business not a job.

He has been a dental advisor providing dental specific coaching, consulting, practice management, and marketing services for over 25 years. Steve's specialties include dental practice management, dental marketing, positioning dental practices to add partners/associates, group practices, and dental team building. His lifelong passion has been helping dentists become transformational leaders to build their dream practice.

At 4M Institute he teaches dentists how to become more profitable, productive, and efficient through effective systems and strategies. Based on his successful coaching and consulting with thousands of dental practices, he also teaches dentists how to significantly increase case acceptance, and masterfully convert patient relationships by phone.

In 1987, Steve fulfilled his lifelong dream of owning his own company and founded Pinnacle Practices, Inc., which grew into the largest dental consulting firm in the South. Over eighteen years, Steve developed in-house programs, teaching strategies, and workshops for his dental clients and worked "hands-on" with thousands of practices, ensuring their success. In addition, Steve lectured regularly at dental schools, dental societies, universities, and study groups and contributed several articles to dental journals and magazines.

In December 2004, Steve sold his company in Dallas, and moved West to Nevada, where he founded Inventive Dental Solutions. Steve has continued and expanded his work coaching clients in Nevada and Southern California and has created the LOTUS Leadership Program for Dental Professionals. Steve has worked hands-on with thousands of practices, developing, and implementing strategic business plans and models for growth and a lifetime of success.

Voted "Best Dental Coach" in 2020.

4M DENTAL IMPLANT CENTER

4M Dental Implant Center provides cleanings, extractions, veneers, Invisalign, and life-changing full-mouth dental implants with our *Full Arch Implant* and *Teeth in One Day* solutions. With thousands of implants placed, the doctors at 4M Dental Implant Center have successfully taken on some of the most complex cases.

4M Full-Mouth Dental Implants are the gold standard for dental implants, a specialized dental implant solution for missing or failing teeth. In a matter of hours, 4M will give you a brand new, healthy, strong, permanent smile.

Our growth continues with locations in Newport Beach, Anaheim, Long Beach, and Las Vegas.

4M INSTITUTE

4M Institute is an educational forum for advancing the dental profession to provide the highest quality clinical, patient, and people outcomes. At 4M Institute's World Headquarters in Long Beach, California, Dr. Sean teaches the art and science of the *Full Arch Implant* and *Teeth in One Day* full mouth dental implant solutions to dentists from around the world.

4M Institute is the leader in continuing dental training for everything from:

- NeoArch to IV-Sedation
- PFR/Phlebotomy
- Leadership Development
- Sales and Marketing for Dentists
- Service Excellence and Patient Satisfaction
- Professional Development for Your Assistants

4M Institute provides CE Credits and registers dentists who successfully complete courses at 4M Institute, as credentialed members of the 4M Certified Dentists' Society.

When you train at 4M Institute, you are getting the best post-graduate, advanced education available, from leading techniques and state-of-the-art equipment to the best trainers and highest tech institution.

By equipping and empowering other dentists, we are changing the lives of many more patients—this is the genesis of the 4M Institute.

4M DENTAL IMPLANT CENTER

4M INSTITUTE

"http://www.4MDentalimplants.com"
www.4MDentalimplants.com
(855)-999-6088

https://4Minstitute.com
(562)-294-5200
3918 Long Beach Blvd. #200
Long Beach, CA 90807

There is a **Personal Action Guide** that accompanies this book.

https://getbook.at/pag_nostandingstill

Made in the USA
Monee, IL
04 November 2026

67384735R00157